W9-AIP-908

# Poland

# Poland

## Second Edition

STEVEN OTFINOSKI

Facts On File, Inc.

Nations in Transition: Poland, Second Edition

Copyright © 2004, 1995 by Steven Otfinoski

Facts On File, Inc.
132 West 31st Street
New York NY 10001

**Library of Congress Cataloging-in-Publication Data**

Otfinoski, Steven.
    Poland / Steven Otfinoski.—2nd ed.
        p. cm.—(Nations in transition)
    Includes bibliographical references and index.
    ISBN 0-8160-5084-8
    1. Poland—History. I. Title. II. Series.
    DK4140.O87 2004
    943.8—dc22                                          2003060074

Facts On File books are available at special discounts when purchased in bulk quantities for businesses, associations, institutions, or sales promotions. Please contact our Special Sales Department in New York at (212) 967-8800 or (800) 322-8755.

You can find Facts On File on the World Wide Web at
http://www.factsonfile.com

Text design by Erika K. Arroyo
Cover design by Nora Wertz
Maps by Dale Williams

MP FOF 10 9 8 7 6 5 4 3 2 1

This book is printed on acid-free paper.

*To Agnes and Jacob, my grandparents*

# CONTENTS

⤳

POLAND

Bornholm
(DENMARK)

Baltic Sea

Pomeranian
Bay

Gulf
of
Gdańsk

LITHUANIA

RUSSIA

GERMANY

BELARUS

UKRAINE

CZECH REPUBLIC

SLOVAKIA

AUSTRIA

HUNGARY

Gdynia
Słupsk
Koszalin
Gdańsk
Braniewo
Elbląg
Tczew
Suwałki
Szczecin
Chojnice
Grudziądz
Iława
Olsztyn
Ełk
Stargard Szczeciński
Wałcz
Bydgoszcz
Toruń
Mława
Łomża
Białystok
Gorzów
Wielkopol
Noteć R.
Piła
Ciechanów
Ostrołęka
Kostryn
Warta R.
Gniezno
Inowrocław
Płock
Bielsk
Podlaski
Słubice
Poznań
Włocławek
Warsaw
Oder R.
Świebodzin
Konin
Kutno
Siedlce
Zielona Góra
Otwock
Biała
Podlaska
Nowa Sól
Leszno
Kalisz
Skierniewice
Żary
Głogów
Ostrów
Wielkopolski
Sieradz
Łódź
Radom
Puławy
Lubin
Piotrków
Trybunalski
Tomaszów
Mazawiecki
Lublin
Bolesławiec
Legnica
Wrocław
Ostrowiec
Świętokrzyski
Chełm
Zgorzelec
Kluczbork
Radomsko
Starachowice
Kraśnik
Zamość
Jelenia Góra
Wałbrzych
Brzeg
Częstochowa
Kielce
Opole
Lubliniec
Jędrzejów
Stalowa
Wolá
Kłodzko
Nysa
Bytom
Sosnowiec
Tarnobrzeg
Mielec
Gliwice
Katowice
Kraków
Rzeszów
Cieszyn
Oświecim
Tarnów
Jarosław
Bielsko-Biała
Krosno
Przemyśl
Sanok
Nowy Targ
Nowy Sącz

Vistula R.
Pisa R.
Biebrza R.
Narew R.
Narew R.
Bug R.
Vistula R.
Oder R.
Warta R.
Vistula R.
San R.

N

0          100 miles
0        100 km

# A Personal Preface

Her name was Agnes. She came from Tarnów, in southwestern Poland, a place that had supported her forefathers for generations. But in the early years of the 20th century, it was no longer a place where she felt she had a future. So, at the age of 18, Agnes left her homeland with a group of friends and relatives and sailed on a passenger ship to America—a land of opportunity for millions of emigrants from Europe.

She settled in New England, in the state of Connecticut. Here, she fell in love with another Polish immigrant, a meat cutter. They married and had a child. Life was good, until one day tragedy struck. Agnes's husband died of tuberculosis. Alone and without friends in a strange land, Agnes returned to Poland with her small son, but not for long. A short time later, she decided to return, convinced she could still find happiness in the United States.

She and her son settled again in Connecticut in the tiny community of Rockfall, where she found work and a room in a boardinghouse that catered to Polish immigrants. It wasn't long before her son caught pneumonia and died. Soon after this, she met another Pole, an ambitious young man named Jacob. They fell in love and married. After suffering an industrial accident that left him blind in one eye, Jacob used the compensation money to buy some farmland in nearby Middletown. Here the couple established a farm, which they worked with their seven children—six boys and a girl. (An eighth child died in a kitchen accident.)

Agnes and Jacob Otfinoski were not extraordinary people. Their hardships and tragedies were shared by millions of immigrants. Yet their story is important to me because they were my grandparents.

The Poland of the grand cities of Warsaw and Kraków and their thousand-year-old culture was not the Poland they had known. Their Poland was a much grimmer place, of overcrowded urban slums and rural areas devastated by famine and the dislocation of war. It was such conditions that drove them and thousands of other working-class Poles to leave their homeland and come to America to find a better life. There they pursued the same trades—farming, mining, manual labor—they had known in Poland. For many of them, their lives became far better than what they had been back home. And their hard work and perseverance promised an even better life for their children.

My Polish heritage was not an important part of my childhood. Unlike my cousins, I did not attend St. Mary's parochial school, where religion and Polish were required subjects. My father, the next to the youngest child, was the only one who moved away from the family homestead after his service in World War II (although he later moved back) and married my mother, a German-American girl, from New York City. My father does not even speak Polish very well. When he spoke Polish around the rest of the family, so the story goes, they would laugh at him.

What I do remember from my childhood are the hearty holiday meals we shared in my grandmother's tiny kitchen on Christmas Eve and Easter. Every Easter, the centerpiece on the dinner table would be a beautifully sculptured lamb made of butter. It was a gift from the good sisters of St. Mary's, the local Polish Catholic church my grandparents helped found.

My grandparents did not instill a strong sense of what it was to be Polish in their children and grandchildren, except by their example. Until the day she died, my grandmother was a devout Catholic, a warm, loving person, and as humble and simple as the Polish soil from whence she came. My grandfather was more distant, but in his younger days, he had been a colorful character—hardworking, hard drinking, and as ambitious to get ahead as any immigrant. He learned how to give haircuts by watching the barber down on Main Street, sold dry goods and homemade whiskey in a general store he ran, and raised horses that he raced on weekends with his Polish friends. For all that happened to them in their new homeland, my grandparents never forgot they were Poles and they never forgot Poland.

Today, the Poles have little reason to want to leave their beloved homeland. With the collapse of communism in 1989 and the establishment of a democratic political system and a free-market economy, Poland, like most of eastern Europe, has become a nation of renewed spirit and hope. But as Poland makes the transition from communism to democracy, new problems and challenges have arisen. This book will examine these challenges as seen through the prism of Poland's past, its land, people, culture, and religion.

# INTRODUCTION

On May 31, 2003, U.S. president George W. Bush stood before a crowd of seven hundred Poles in the courtyard of Kraków's great Wawel Royal Castle. "You . . . struggled to become a full member of the Atlantic alliance," Bush said in his speech. "Yet you have not come all this way, through occupation and tyranny and brave uprisings, only to be told that you must now choose between Europe and America. [Poland] is a good citizen of Europe, and Poland is a good friend of America, and there is no conflict between the two."

When Bush said "Europe," he was not referring to Russia, or the former Soviet Union that controlled Poland for more than 40 years. He was speaking of western Europe—particularly France and Germany—which has been critical of Poland's wholehearted support of the United States and the American-led invasion of Iraq in March 2003 that toppled the dictatorship of Saddam Hussein.

Polish troops went into Iraq as part of the coalition, just as they had joined American troops the year before in Afghanistan to overthrow the repressive Taliban regime and the terrorists of al-Qaeda whom the Taliban were harboring.

The nations of western Europe, with only a few exceptions, notably Great Britain, have not supported the Iraqi war, and in this time of shifting alliances, Poland has become one of the United States' staunchest allies in Europe.

"America will not forget that Poland rose to the moment," Bush noted in Kraków. It is telling that in a European tour that included stops in Russia and France, Bush started his trip by visiting Poland.

The praise of a U.S. president is only one indication that Poland is becoming a major player in the changing face of Europe. This country, which 200 years ago had virtually vanished from the map of Europe, is today one of the strongest nations in eastern Europe and economically positioned to become one of the powerhouses of all of Europe in the 21st century.

Poland's political and economic ties to the United States are vital to that success, but despite European criticism, its clout on the continent has come a long way in the decade and a half since it won independence from the Soviet Union. As the economic organization of 15 nations—the European Union (EU)—prepares to admit Poland and nine other nations to its ranks in May 2004, it has paid the most respect and given the most concessions to Poland, and for good reason. Poland is by far the largest of the new members, both in land size and population. It will offer the largest market for goods to EU members and have the most exports to offer in return.

Despite many setbacks on the road to a free-market economy and a democratic government, Poland is getting ready to take its place of leadership in a newly aligned Europe. While it still may have a long way to go, it has already made tremendous strides. Given its long history of wars, invasions, and foreign occupations, this achievement is even more impressive.

# Geography

It has been said that in the world's history, geography determines destiny. The United States—separated from Europe and Asia by two mighty oceans and graced with a temperate climate, abundant natural resources, and peaceful nonthreatening neighbors to the north and south—has developed into one of the world's mightiest superpowers. Few countries on Earth have been so blessed with good geography as the United States. Few countries have been as poorly served by geography as Poland.

Located in the heart of Europe, Poland is mostly a flat, fertile plain with no mountains, rivers, or other natural obstacles to the west or east to protect it from its powerful neighbors—Germany to the west and Russia to the east. In its thousand-year history, Poland has been the victim of countless invasions, not just from these two nations, but from the Mongols to the east, the Swedes to the north, and the Turks and Czechs to the south.

But Poland has not always been so vulnerable. There was a time, between invasions and defeat, when Poland was one of the most powerful nations in Europe. Since that "golden age," however, Poland has been conquered, divided, partitioned, and finally gobbled up by its greedy neighbors so that it no longer existed as an independent country.

This curse of geography may be expected to have produced a people who are weak, vacillating, and cowardly, but the Poles are a strong, proud people with a rich and age-old culture. The blows that fate has dealt them over the centuries have ennobled their character and made them resilient, enduring, and resourceful. Their very lack of freedom has made the Poles cling all the more fiercely to the ideal of freedom and its fruits. Few nationalities are more deserving of the name "freedom fighters" than the Polish people. Deprived of their very country for over a century, they kept it alive in their hearts. Through pogroms, repressions, failed rebellions, and the threat of total extinction in the 20th century, Poles kept hope alive as expressed in the opening words of their national anthem:

> Poland has not perished yet
> So long as we still live.

But there is also a dark side to this national character. Poland's love of freedom has, in the past, paradoxically been the very instrument by which the nation has lost it. Dissent and disagreement have led to internal conflict and political chaos, further aggravated by a long tradition of self-interest among the highborn and wealthy. For centuries, the Polish nobility refused to give up their power for national unity and the good of the country. Romantic and idealistic in their quest for independence, Poles have historically failed time and again to turn those ideals into political realities. As novelist James Michener has written, "Personal freedom was the lifeblood of Poland but the supreme irony was that its freedom-loving citizens were not able to develop those governmental forms which would preserve that freedom."

Like so many of the great nations of the world, Poland is a mass of contradictions—a freedom-loving people too often ill equipped to handle freedom, a downtrodden country that has never given up hope, a land of a devoutly religious people who lived for 40 years under the atheistic

*Sheep graze peacefully on this hillside in Poland's Vistula Valley. The Vistula River is one of Europe's longest and most naturally beautiful waterways.* (Courtesy Free Library of Philadelphia)

regime of communism. To understand Poland better, it is necessary to look closely at the land itself, its people, resources, and geographical regions. Although dominated by flat plains, on a closer look, Poland is surprisingly diversified geographically.

# The Seven Land Regions

Poland is the second-largest country in eastern Europe. Only Russia is bigger. Its landmass, enlarged and shrunken by countless wars and border disputes, is presently 120,725 square miles (312,678 km), roughly the size of the British Isles or the state of New Mexico.

Poland is bordered on the north by the Baltic Sea, beyond which lies Sweden. To the south are the rugged Carpathian Mountains and the Czech Republic and Slovakia. To the west is Germany and to the east, Russia.

From north to south, Poland has seven distinct regions. Along the Baltic coast, Poland's only access to the sea, is a narrow strip of sun-filled beaches and pleasant resorts that is called the Polish Riviera. On either end of this sandy stretch are two natural harbors, home to the important port cities of Szczecin and Gdańsk. The workers of Gdańsk are an independent and defiant breed, and Polish freedom was reborn through their efforts in the 1980s under the banner of the Solidarity movement.

Below the coastal lowlands is a broader swath of land known as the Lakes Region. Foreigners surprised to find Poland has a Riviera may be equally surprised to discover this wooded region dotted with 7,703 lakes. Formed largely by prehistoric glaciers, many of these small lakes are joined by rivers and canals, allowing vacationers to sail or canoe along the pristine waterways for many miles. The Lakes Region's primary industry is tourism. The Poles who live here are proud of the natural beauty of their land and are eager to share it with visitors. Their hospitality, something a tourist experiences everywhere in Poland, is best expressed by the old Polish proverb "A guest in the home, God in the home."

The forests and lakes teem with wildlife, including swans and cranes and the largest herd of elk found in Europe. Lumbering is also important, although farming is limited mostly to rye and potatoes.

Below the Lakes Region are the Central Plains, the heart of Poland. Long the stomping grounds of Poland's enemies, this flat, green plain is covered by thousands of farms and the great Polish cities of Poznań, Wrocław, Łódź, and Warsaw, the capital. The reawakening of life, often grim under communism, can perhaps best be seen in one of the region's poorer cities, such as Białystok, which lies northeast of Warsaw. New construction and freshly painted buildings are brightening the once-gray urban landscape. "Look around," Deputy Mayor Ewa Bonczak-Kucharczyk told a foreign reporter. "This place is booming with construction." But her pride was mixed with scorn for the new government responsible for the changes. "The Democratic Left Alliance [made up mostly of former Communists] is rather better at spending money than investing."

Life has changed less for the farming families in the countryside. They continue to work the hard soil, less fertile than in other regions, to make it produce sugar beets, rye, potatoes, and other crops.

The region is transversed by Poland's two great river systems: the Bug-Vistula-Notec-Warta system and the Oder-Warta and Odra system. The

Vistula is the country's single longest river, rising in the Carpathian Mountains in the south, flowing across the plains and emptying into the Baltic Sea, 675 miles (1,086 km) away from its source.

Among the natural preserves located in this region is Białowieza National Park, whose 312,000 acres (125,000 hectares) straddle Poland and Russia. A national park since 1919, Białowieza is Europe's only remaining primeval forest and home to the largest herd of bison in the world. The story of Poland's bison illustrates a resiliency that matches that of its people.

Once protected by Polish royalty in their hunting grounds, the bison dwindled in recent centuries and were completely killed off and eaten by starving soldiers in World War I. In 1929, three pairs of native bison were brought in from European zoos and returned to their natural habitat. They multiplied and numbered 250 by the mid-1980s. The Poles have since returned the favor and now send their bison to zoos and preserves across the globe to start new herds.

Just south of the plains are the Polish Uplands, consisting of rolling hills and lofty mountains. This well-populated area is rich in fertile farmland and mineral deposits. Uplands farms are found mostly in the east and produce wheat, corn, and potatoes. The region around the city of Katowice contains one of the world's largest coalfields, where generations of Polish workers have gone down into the mines for a living. Coal is Poland's most precious natural resource, and it is the world's sixth-largest producer of coal. Other minerals found in the Uplands include copper, lead, and zinc, while the city of Oppela is famous for its cement industry.

South of the Polish Uplands is a narrow belt known as the Carpathian Forelands. The region's fertile soil supports many farms and a dense population. Its major city is the ancient and venerable Kraków, home to Poland's oldest university. Outside Kraków is Nowa Huta, center of Poland's steel and iron industries.

Forming Poland's southern border is the Western Carpathian Mountains district. Their tallest peak, Rysy, rises to more than 8,000 feet (2,499 m), the nation's highest point above sea level. A popular vacation spot, the Carpathians are thick with forests and include several national parks. The Highlanders who live here are a hardy, independent people instantly identifiable by their colorful folk costumes and the *ciupagi,* a mountaineer's cane with an ax handle, they carry. Their traditional homes, made of mountain timber, are as unique as they are.

Tucked away in the southwest corner of Poland is the seventh geographical region, the Sudetes Mountains. These lower peaks rise to under 5,000 feet (1,500 m) above sea level and are older than the Carpathians. The cities and towns of this region are home to a thriving textile industry.

The Polish climate varies from region to region but is generally milder at the coast than inland and colder in the mountains than the plains and lowlands. January temperatures average 26°F (-3°C) and 73°F (23°C) in July.

It has often been said that we love most in life what we have lost. The Poles have lost their cherished land with its mountains and forests and plains and lakes many times in their turbulent history. It is that history that has shaped their character, defined their present, and given them hope and determination as they face a promising, but still uncertain, future.

## NOTES

p. xiii "'You . . . struggled to become . . .'" *New York Times*, June 1, 2003, p. 1.

p. xiii "'America will not forget . . .'" *New York Times*, June 1, 2003, p. 14.

p. xv "'Poland has not perished yet . . .'" Norman Davies. *God's Playground: A History of Poland*, vol. 2. (New York: Columbia University Press, 1982), p. 16.

p. xv "'Personal freedom was the lifeblood . . .'" James Michener. *Poland* (New York: Fawcett Crest, 1984), p. 53.

p. xvii "'A guest in the home . . .'" "Poland Invites." Brochure of Polish Tourist Information Center.

p. xvii "'Look around . . .'" *New York Times*, October 3, 1993, p. 14.

# PART I
# History

# 1

# THE RISE AND FALL OF POLAND (PREHISTORY TO 1918)

According to legend, an ancient tribe led by three brothers once wandered across what is now the continent of Europe. One day they entered a land of unsurpassing beauty. One brother, Lech, saw an eagle in its nest and took it as a good omen. "This is where we should settle," he said to his brothers, Czech and Rus.

They disagreed with him and the tribe split into three groups, each led by one brother. Czech took his tribe westward and settled what later became Czechoslovakia. Rus went east and settled what is today Russia. Lech and his tribe stayed in what was to became Poland. He founded a city on the spot where he saw the eagle and called it Gniezno, "nest" in Polish. Gniezno later became the first capital of Poland and is today a thriving city. The white eagle became the symbol of Lech's tribe and remains the symbol of Poland to this day.

This fanciful tale may be legend, but it contains more than a germ of truth. The earliest people to inhabit eastern Europe were Slavic tribes, and they originally settled in the thick forests of Poland and western Russia about 2000 B.C. From this base they spread out, gradually settling in what is today the Czech Republic, Slovakia, the Balkans, Greece, and Germany.

One of the largest Slavic tribes in Poland was the Polanie, which literally means "people who live in the field." They called the land they lived in Poland. In their primitive communities called *grody*, the Polanie and their neighbors cultivated grains, raised domestic animals, and established a simple form of government run by tribal chieftains. Gradually their little communities grew into towns and cities. One of these *grody* eventually became the city of Poznań in west-central Poland, the nation's oldest continually inhabited city.

## Poland's First Dynasty—The Piasts

The Polanie came to dominate the other tribes and organized them into separate individual states. The first great Polanie ruler was the legendary Piast, of whom little is known other than that he founded Poland's first dynasty of kings. Piast's great-great-grandson, Mieszko I, is the first historic prince of Poland. He ruled from A.D. 963 to 992 and is known for two great accomplishments: uniting the tribes of Poland into a nation and accepting Christianity for his country.

Mieszko's religious conversion was partially political. Although a separate country, Poland was under the domination of the German Teutonic tribes to the west. By accepting Christianity, Mieszko could count on protection against the Germans from the Holy Roman Empire, an empire in western-central Europe founded by Charlemagne, king of the Franks, in 800.

The Roman Catholic Church also brought Western culture to Poland, putting it on a different path of development from Russia and other neighboring countries, which developed traditions more Eastern than Western.

Mieszko's son Bolesław the Brave, who succeeded him as prince of Great Poland in 992, was an even more adept ruler than his father. He strengthened the ties among the tribes under him, made peace with the Germans who were still a threat, and extended Poland's territory. In 1000, he was crowned first king of Poland by Holy Roman emperor Otto III. As often happens in hereditary monarchies, Bolesław's sons did not have his gift for state building. After his death in 1025, they quarreled among themselves for power and carved Poland up into small kingdoms. Unable to defend themselves, these kingdoms courted disaster. Over the defenseless plains rode a series of invaders—Germans, Russians, Czechs, and most dreaded of all, the Mongolian Tatars.

These invaders often left total devastation in their path. Novelist James Michener described a Tatar attack on a Polish village in 1241 in his historical novel *Poland:*

> Like an explosion of lava from a volcano, the horsemen swept over the settlement, setting fire to every cottage, slaying every human being they encountered, even killing cattle too old to be herded easily to that night's campsite, wherever it was going to be. Of those Bukowo peasants trapped inside the village, all were slain, even though not one of them had taken arms against the Tatars or tried in any way to oppose them.

By the early 1300s, however, two strong leaders emerged to reunify a people who now shared a common language and religion. Władysław the Short (reigned 1306–33) and his son Casimir the Great (1333–70) reformed the Polish kingdom and helped shape its culture by encouraging the arts. Casimir, who established a single system of money and founded the University of Kraków, is today considered one of Poland's greatest kings. An old saying claims, "He found a Poland made of wood and left behind one made of stone."

Casimir died without an heir and was therefore the last of the Piast kings. His kingdom fell into the hands of his nephew, King Louis of Hungary. Louis had little interest in Poland or its people and ruled with benign neglect. He had no sons, and the Polish nobles, fearing they would face political chaos on his death, made an unusual decision. They demanded that Louis's nine-year-old daughter Jadwiga (see boxed biography) succeed him as Poland's ruler. Two years later Louis died and Jadwiga was crowned "king" in Kraków, one of the few female monarchs in modern European history.

What followed is a star-crossed romance out of a fairy tale. Jadwiga was in love with an Austrian prince named Wilhelm, but Poland's nobles decided on a more politically useful mate for her. Neighboring Lithuania, on the Baltic coast, was at war with Poland, and the Polish nobles wanted to make peace between the two countries and join them against a common enemy—the Teutonic Knights of Germany. To this end they forced Jadwiga to give up Wilhelm and become engaged to Grand Duke Władysław Jagiełło of Lithuania. Jadwiga was 12 and the grand duke 32 at the time. For the good of her country, Jadwiga agreed to the marriage. On his part, Jagiełło agreed to accept Christianity.

# Poland's Golden Age

Jagiełło proved to be a good husband and an even better ruler. Although Jadwiga died in 1399, Jagiełło ruled Poland as Władysław II for another 35 years. In 1410 he led the Poles and Lithuanians in one of the great military victories of medieval Europe, defeating the Teutonic Knights in the Battle of Grünwald.

He described the memorable battle in a letter to his second wife, Anna of Cilli:

> On Tuesday, the Feast of the Apostles, the Grand Master [of the Teutonic Knights] with all his power drew close to your forces, and demanded that battle be joined. . . . After we had stood and watched

---

## QUEEN JADWIGA (1370–1399)

She is considered by many to be the Polish Joan of Arc, although she never led an army into battle and did not die a martyr to a cause. She might in fact have ended up merely the pawn in an international game of power politics, but thanks to her strength of character and deep love for her country she became much more than that.

Jadwiga was a princess by birth, daughter of Louis the Great of Hungary and Elizabeth of Bosnia. Her father had inherited the Polish throne and treated his distant subjects with indifference. The Poles wanted a ruler to follow Louis who would be their own and pressured the Hungarian monarch, who had no sons, to enlist one of his daughters as their next "king." Jadwiga got the job by default—one elder sister died and the other was being groomed for the Hungarian throne.

Leaving her homeland for a new and strange country was only Jadwiga's first sacrifice for Poland. A political marriage to Grand Duke Jogaila (Jagiełło in Polish) of Lithuania was the second. The joining of Poland and Lithuania strengthened both countries and helped create a Polish empire that would flourish for nearly two centuries.

Although her marriage to Władysław II Jagiełło reduced Jadwiga's power as monarch, she continued to corule with him and was

each other for a time, the Grand Master sent two swords over to us with this message: "Know you, King . . . , that this very hour we shall do battle with you. For this, we send you these swords for your assistance." We replied: "We accept the swords you send us, and in the name of Christ, before whom all stiff-necked pride must bow, we shall do battle." At which, with the troops standing in full order, we advanced to the fray without delay. Among the numberless dead, we ourselves had few losses. . . . We cut down the Grand Master, . . . forcing many others to flee. . . . The pursuit continued for two miles. Many were drowned in the lakes and rivers, and many killed, so that very few escaped. . . .

Jagiełło's victory secured his power and created a new dynasty of Jagiellonian kings who ruled Poland for about 200 years. This period from

his wisest counselor. Her two greatest achievements as queen were negotiating a peaceful settlement with the warlike Teutonic Knights to the west and the rebuilding of the University of Kraków, which had been founded by her great-uncle, Casimir the Great.

The birth of her son in 1399 was a joyful event, producing the first male heir to the Polish throne in decades. Tragically, the child died, and Jadwiga, weak and despondent, died soon after at the age of 29. She did not live to see her beloved university reopen nor the great flowering of Polish culture under her husband's dynasty, yet she is still remembered today as a woman of great faith, gentleness, and peace.

*Queen Jadwiga was a woman of great dignity and determination, as revealed in this portrait.*
(Courtesy Library of Congress)

---

## NICOLAUS COPERNICUS (MIKOŁAJ KOPERNIK) (1473–1543)

The man known as "The Father of Astronomy" was born in the city of Toruń (or Thorn in German) in north-central Poland. His father died when he was 10, and he was raised by an uncle, who was a city cathedral official and later a bishop of the Catholic Church. The church appeared to be the career path for Copernicus as well, although he became seriously interested in astronomy during his student days at Jagiellonian University in Kraków.

Most astronomers still accepted the 1,300-year-old theory of the Greek scientist Ptolemy, which said Earth was the unmovable center of the universe and that all the heavenly bodies moved around it. Copernicus, however, believed this was untrue. He spent his life proving, by observation of the Moon and planets, that Earth, like the other planets, rotated around the Sun.

After his studies, Copernicus was appointed by his uncle as the canon, or head clergyman, of Warmia Cathedral in Frombork, Poland. A man of indefatigable energy, he managed to perform his church duties while working on his astronomical experiments and earning a degree as a medical doctor. In his spare time Copernicus developed Poland's first standard currency to fight growing inflation. His plan was, unfortunately, rejected by the government.

Copernicus knew full well that the church and state would be even less tolerant of an attack on Ptolemy's theory, which kept humankind at the center of the universe. He wisely kept his own the-

---

1410 to 1572 is known as Poland's Golden Age, and for good reason. Under the Jagiellonians, Poland grew from a nation-state to an empire. Poland controlled the rich Ukraine, a province of Russia, and other Russian lands. Polish art and literature reached new heights.

The Jagiellonians established a national parliament called the Sejm in 1493, the year after Columbus reached America, making Poland one of the first European countries to establish democratic traditions. Twelve years later it adopted a constitution, granting limited rights to all Polish citizens. This "democracy" was a far cry from the democracy enjoyed in the United States and other countries today. The Sejm was selected by the king and nobility from their own numbers. But this first important step

ory a secret while writing down his ideas in a book called *De Revolutionibus Orbium Coelestium*, Latin for "Concerning the revolutions of the celestial spheres." When news of his book and its revolutionary theory leaked out, Copernicus, then an old man of 70, finally agreed to have it published. He saw the finished book on his deathbed. Copernicus's book blazed the way for such modern astronomers as Galileo Galilei and Johannes Kepler to probe the stars and planets.

"The theory of the Earth's motion is admittedly difficult to comprehend," Copernicuswrote in his great work. "But if God wills, I shall . . . make it clearer than the Sun . . ." He did, shedding light on the universe and ushering in the modern scientific age.

*"The Father of Astronomy,"* Copernicus divided his life between science and the church, where he served as a high clergyman. His theory that placed the Sun, not Earth, at the center of the solar system was controversial, and he agreed to publish his findings only near the end of his life. (Courtesy Free Library of Philadelphia)

toward representative government was far more advanced than any taken by the monarchies that then existed in France, Germany, and Russia.

This new freedom, however, had its downside. If even one member of the Sejm disagreed with a proposed law, all he had to do was stand up and say *"nei pozevlom"* (I disapprove), and the law could not pass. This prevented most laws from ever passing and often reduced the parliament to a quarreling, ineffective body. Nevertheless, the nobles jealously guarded what power they had and a fatal pattern of weak, ineffective kings emerged that would bode ill for the nation in the years ahead.

When Sigismund Augustus II, another childless monarch, died in 1572, the nobles of the Sejm decided that rather than let one of their own number become king, they would elect a foreign king. A foreigner, they reasoned, would be lax in his long-distance rule and allow them more room to exert their own authority. So in 1587, Sigismund III Vasa, king of Sweden, became king of Poland. It was a grave mistake that signaled the end of the Golden Age and started Poland on a downward spiral that would continue for centuries.

## The Long Decline

Poor leadership, internal squabbling, and wars with its neighbors weakened the Polish government until it was unable to govern its empire. The Ukrainians rebelled in 1648 and won their independence from Poland. In 1655 Sweden grasped control of Poland's Baltic provinces. But then a common enemy united the rivaling states. The Islamic Turks advanced into Poland, intent on taking it over along with the rest of central Europe.

King John III Sobieski (reigned 1674–96), one of Poland's strongest rulers in the 17th century, led a brazen assault against the Turks in Austria at the historic Battle of Vienna in 1683. He dealt them a resounding defeat that saved not only Poland but also all of Europe from Turkish rule. It was one of Europe's most decisive battles; however, it did not save Poland from its other enemies. When Sobieski died in 1696, the Sejm elected its next king from German Saxony. This incensed the descendants of Sobieski, who won the support of Poland's neighbors in the War of the Polish Succession (1733–35). This war, in which Polish soldiers played only a marginal role, ended in victory for the Saxon king Augustus III.

## The Three Partitions

By greedily keeping power unto themselves, the Sejm once again brought their country to the brink of disaster. By 1772 Russia, Austria, and Prussia, the largest of the German states, made a treaty to seize a chunk of Poland for each of them. Russia took part of eastern Poland, which became Belorussia. Austria grabbed much of southern Poland. Prussia took the section known as Pomerania in western Poland. Together, the three took a third of Poland's territory and half of its people in what has come to be called the First Partition.

*A commander in the Ottoman Turkish army prepares to lead his soldiers into the Battle of Vienna in 1683. The Turks were defeated by the army of Poland's King John III Sobieski, thereby ending Turkish plans to conquer Europe.* (Courtesy Library of Congress)

The Poles rose angrily against their enemies. In 1791 the government produced a new constitution that ended the Sejm's "liberum vote," granted more personal freedoms, and gave the vote to many more Poles. It was a much-needed reform, but it came too late. Poland no longer had the military might or strong leadership to save itself from its more powerful neighbors. In fact, the reforms actually hastened the country's downfall. The monarchies of Russia and Prussia feared Poland's democratic reforms might spread to their own countries. In 1793 the Second Partition of Poland saw these two countries carve up more of the nation to the west and the east.

The Poles rose up in arms the following year to take back their territory. They were led by the courageous general Tadeusz Kościuszko (see boxed biography), who had fought in the American Revolution 15 years earlier. Like many uprisings in Poland before and since, the rebellion of 1794 was a valiant effort but a doomed one. Outnumbered and outweaponed, the Poles lost and Kościuszko was captured and imprisoned by the Russians.

The following year the process that began more than two decades earlier drew to its bitter conclusion. Russia, Prussia, and Austria divided the remains of the Polish state among themselves. The population of the Polish lands, which included Lithuania, had shrunk from 14 million at the time of the First Partition to a mere 6 million at the time of the Third Partition.

## TADEUSZ KOŚCIUSZKO (1746–1817)

"He is as pure a son of liberty as I have ever known," said Thomas Jefferson of this Polish nobleman who fought for freedom on two continents.

Tadeusz Andrzei Bonawentura Kościuszko was born into an old but poor noble family and studied at the Royal Military School in Warsaw. His ambition was to be a soldier, and he went to France to study military engineering. When he returned to Poland in 1774, he worked as a tutor for the daughter of a Cossack leader. The romantic young man fell in love with his student and barely escaped her father's wrath with his life.

He fled to France and then America, a land in as much turmoil as Poland. The cause of American freedom from Britain moved Kościuszko deeply, and he offered his services as a volunteer to the Philadelphia Congress. They immediately made him a colonel of engineers. Kościuszko's contribution to the American Revolution was critical. He helped win the Battle of Saratoga with a brilliant defense plan, designed and built the fortress at West Point, which still stands, and served as chief engineer of the Continental Army's southern forces. For his loyal service he was rewarded at the war's end with land, an annual pension, the rank of brigadier general, and United States citizenship.

Kościuszko returned to Poland in 1784, hoping to see his land win the same freedom his adopted country had. He fought in the war of 1791, which ended in Poland's defeat and the loss of much of its territory.

Three years later Kościuszko led against the Russians the valiant insurrection that bears his name. Leading peasants wielding scythes, he beat the Russians at Raclawice on April 4, 1794. But the Russians outnumbered

Poland ceased to exist as a political entity. It disappeared from the map of Europe. Its neighbors had obliterated a country that had existed for a thousand years.

## A Nation of Exiles

But the Polish people would not be obliterated so easily. They kept the flame of Polish freedom burning in their minds and hearts, both at home and abroad, where many went during these difficult years. Throughout

the Poles and defeat once again was inevitable. The Third Partition made Poland disappear entirely from the map of Europe. Kościuszko was wounded and captured at the bloody Battle of Maciejowice in October. He was imprisoned in St. Petersburg's Peter and Paul Fortress for three years. Czar Paul I pardoned the Pole in 1797, and Kościuszko traveled to London, a man without a country.

Kościuszko returned to the United States, where he collected his accumulating pension and used it to finance plans for Polish independence. Back in Europe he raised support for the struggle but received little encouragement. A broken, lonely man, Kościuszko settled in Switzerland, where he died at age 71. In his will he asked that his lands in America be sold and the money used to buy black Americans out of slavery. It was the final legacy of a man who believed passionately in the cause of freedom for all people.

*A dashing figure, as seen here in his military garb, Tadeusz Kościuszko was called the "Hero of Two Worlds" because of his involvement in the American Revolution and the insurrection he later led in his native Poland.* (Courtesy Free Library of Philadelphia)

the 19th century they kept the idea of Poland alive through their art, music, and literature, most notably in the passionate, patriotic piano compositions of Frédéric Chopin (see boxed biography, chapter 7) and the stirring poetry of Adam Bernard Mickiewicz (1798–1855). Perhaps no Pole better expressed the defiant spirit of his conquered nation than Mickiewicz when he wrote these words:

Poland said: "Whosoever will come to me shall be free and equal, for I am FREEDOM." But the Kings when they heard were frightened in their hearts, and said . . . "Come, let us slay this nation." And they conspired together . . . And they crucified the Polish Nation, and laid it in its grave, and cried out "We have slain and buried Freedom." But they cried out foolishly . . .

For the Polish Nation did not die. Its body lieth in the grave, but its spirit has descended into the abyss, that is into the private lives of people who suffer slavery in their country . . . But on the third day the soul shall return again to the body, and the Nation shall arise, and free all the peoples of Europe from slavery.

For a brief moment, the Poles' romantic idealism found a champion in the century's first great figure, French ruler and conqueror Napoléon Bonaparte. With expatriate soldiers in his ranks, Napoléon recaptured Polish lands taken by Prussia and "returned" them to the Poles under the name of the Grand Duchy of Warsaw. But, in fact, Napoléon controlled the Grand Duchy in all but name. In the end it was just another one of his conquests. After his fall from power in 1815, the land returned to Prussia. As a kind of cruel joke, the Russians decided to name one part of their Polish lands the "Kingdom of Poland," but it remained in firm Russian control.

Among Poland's three masters, only Austria allowed the Poles to keep their language and culture. Russia and Prussia mercilessly suppressed the Polish way of life among its people. Polish schools were strictly run by their foreign overlords. The daughter of Manya Skłodowska, who would later become world famous as the Nobel Prize-winning chemist Madame Curie, describes a visit from a Russian inspector to her mother's school in Warsaw in 1878:

M. Hornberg, accepting the chair offered him by Mlle Tupalska, seated himself heavily.

"Please call on one of these young people."

In the third row Manya Sklodovska instinctively turned her frightened little face toward the window. . . .

But she knew very well that the choice would fall upon her. She knew that she was almost always chosen for the government inspector's questioning. . . .

At the sound of her name, she straightened up. . . .

"Your prayer," snapped M. Hornberg . . .

Manya recited "Our Father" in a voice without color or expression. One of the subtlest humiliations the Tsar [Russia's king] had discovered was to make the Polish children say their Catholic prayers every day *in Russian*. . . .

"Who rules over us?"

To conceal the fire of their eyes, the directress and the superintendent stared hard at the registers they held before them. As the answer did not come quickly enough, Hornberg, annoyed, asked again in louder tones:

"Who rules over us?"

"His Majesty Alexander II, Tsar of All the Russias," Manya articulated painfully. Her face had gone white.

The Poles were not always able to "conceal the fire" they felt inside. There were uprisings in 1830, 1840, and 1863—all of which failed.

## World War I and Independence

As the 19th century drew to a close, however, a new and charismatic Polish leader named Józef Piłsudski emerged. Piłsudski, a Socialist, spent five years in exile in Siberia for agitating. In 1892 he returned to Russian Poland and founded a left-wing, patriotic newspaper, *Robotnik* (The Worker). When World War I broke out in 1914, Piłsudski led a legion of 10,000 Polish troops who fought on the Austrian side against the Russians. Piłsudski became a national hero but was interned by the Germans, the Austrians' allies, in 1917 because they did not trust him. This led the Poles to the grim realization that despite the different sides Austria, Germany, and Russia fought on, they were still united in their oppression of Poland.

In 1918 Germany and Austria lost the war. The empire they had built up over two centuries fell to pieces. Roman Dmowski, another Polish leader, founded a Polish National Committee in Paris. He lobbied fervently for the Allied powers of the United States, France, and England to help form an independent Poland.

The Americans were deeply sympathetic to the Polish cause. Many Poles had immigrated to America in the late 1800s and early 1900s and had contributed greatly to their new homeland. U.S. president Woodrow Wilson made Polish independence one of the conditions of the armistice treaty. Piłsudski was chosen to head up the new and independent Poland. After nearly 125 years of subjugation, a new Poland emerged from the ashes of the Great War. The future held great promise, but it also held great challenges.

## NOTES

p. 5 "'Like an explosion of lava . . .'" James Michener. *Poland* (New York: Fawcett Crest, 1984), p. 40.

p. 5 "'He found a Poland made of wood . . .'" Christine Pfeiffer. *Poland—Land of Freedom Fighters* (New York: Columbia University Press, 1982), p. 123.

pp. 6–7 "'On Tuesday . . .'" Norman Davies. *God's Playground*, vol. 1 (New York: Columbia University Press, 1982), p. 123.

p. 9 "'The theory of the Earth's motion . . .'" Arnold Madison. *Polish Greats* (New York: David McKay Co., 1980), p. 8.

p. 12 "'He is as pure a son . . .'" Carole Greene. *Poland* (Chicago: Children's Press, 1983), p. 101.

p. 14 "'Poland said: "Whosoever will come to me" . . .'" Davies, vol. 1, pp. 8–9.

pp. 14–15 "'M. Hornberg, accepting the chair . . .'" Eve Curie. *Madame Curie*, translated by Vincent Sheean (New York: Da Capo Press, 1986), pp. 19–21.

# 2

# POLAND UNDER DEMOCRACY, NAZISM, AND COMMUNISM (1918 TO 1980)

Poland was a free country again after more than a century of foreign domination, but independence brought a new host of problems. Putting Poland back together was a little like putting Humpty Dumpty back together. The Allies helped Poland reclaim territory from Germany and Austria, but Russia, now controlled by the Communists after the Russian Revolution of 1917, refused to turn over its Polish lands. The conflict quickly led to war.

"By attacking Poland," reasoned Russian leader Vladimir Lenin, "we are attacking also the Allies. By destroying the Polish army we are destroying the Versailles settlement." It was, however, the Soviets who were defeated in the short war, and under the Treaty of Riga, signed in 1921, Russia returned at least some of its Polish territory.

The new Polish republic declared its lofty ideals in the invocation to its new constitution, which was passed on March 17, 1921:

We, the people of Poland, thanking Providence for freeing us from one and a half centuries of servitude, remembering with gratitude the bravery, endurance, and selfless struggles of past generations, which unceasingly devoted all their best energies to the cause of Independence . . . striving for the welfare of the whole, united, and independent mother-country, and for her sovereign existence, might, security, and social order, and desiring to ensure the development of all moral and material powers for the good of the whole of regenerated mankind and to ensure the equality of all citizens, respect for labour, all due rights, and particularly the security of State protection, we hereby proclaim and vote this Constitutional Statute in the Legislative Assembly of the Republic of Poland.

Achieving these goals, however, would not be easy. A century of separation had made Poles in the three partitioned sections strangers to one another. The ideal of a free Poland was something they had yearned and fought for for decades. Now that it had become a reality, that chronic reluctance to give up individual independence for the good of all once again asserted itself. According to a 1931 census, a little less than 70 percent of the population was Polish. The remaining inhabitants were Ukrainian, Jewish, Belorussian, and German. They clamored for recognition and more rights.

It was a daunting challenge, even for a strong leader like Józef Piłsudski, to get these diverse groups to agree on anything. In its first eight years, the new Poland had no fewer than 13 different governments, each appointed by an increasingly disillusioned Piłsudski. The economy was also in shambles—antiquated, ineffective, and unjust. Three-quarters of the population worked in agriculture and were mostly peasant farmers. Industrial workers in cities made up only 17 percent of the population. The remaining tiny percentage—professionals, entrepreneurs, and landowners—held all the wealth and power.

# From Democracy to Dictatorship

In 1923 Piłsudski resigned in disgust as premier. Three years later he led a military coup and marched into Warsaw, taking the city. The watchword of his coup was *sanacja*—a moral "cleansing" of the state that would end corruption, limit the power of the Sejm, and strengthen the power of the executive branch of government. On May 31, 1926, Piłsudski was elected president of Poland. In effect, he became his country's dictator.

If Piłsudski was a dictator, however, he was a relatively benign one. He used his power to stabilize the economy, secure the state, and improve relations with other nations. His goodwill campaign culminated in a loan of $172 million in 1929 from the West, most of it from the United States.

Piłsudski remained in power until his death at 68 in May 1935. One of his last acts was to adopt a new constitution that limited the powers

*German troops parade triumphantly through the streets of Warsaw after the invasion in September 1939, which ignited World War II.* (Courtesy National Archives)

## IGNACY JAN PADEREWSKI (1860–1941)

Hearing the young Polish pianist play, the celebrated Viennese piano teacher Theodor Leschetizky said, "It is too late. Your fingers lack discipline. You can never become a great pianist." But the young Pole believed otherwise. Ignacy Jan Paderewski worked hard and in three years embarked on a career as a concert pianist that would make him one of the world's most renowned virtuosos.

In 1891 Paderewski made his first memorable concert tour of the United States. He would return 19 times. Outside of playing the piano, his passions were billiards, bridge, and the cause of Polish independence.

Paderewski gave away so much of his wealth to worthy causes, including the Polish nationalistic movement, that he had to come out of semiretirement and return to public playing to make money, in spite of a serious nervous disorder. During World War I he toured North and South America, raising money for his war-racked country.

"I came to speak to you of a nation which is not yours," he would declare to spellbound audiences, "in a language which is not mine." It was Paderewski who personally persuaded U.S. president Woodrow Wilson to include independence for Poland in his Fourteen Points for a peace treaty.

of the president. His successors found it more difficult to keep control of the country, which soon was beset by protests and strikes. Polish communists and right-wing conservatives struggled for power, leaving little room for the moderate leaders to maneuver. Meanwhile, events outside Poland were taking an even more ominous turn.

After a decade of economic ruin and political flux following its defeat in World War I, Germany had chosen a new leader who promised a brighter future—Adolf Hitler. Hitler rebuilt German economic and military strength through the mid-1930s. In 1938 he demanded that Poland return the port city of Gdańsk, which had previously been the German city of Danzig. Poland refused. Hitler now had the excuse he had been looking for to go to war.

When the war finally ended, the distinguished Pole was chosen to be his country's premier and minister of foreign affairs. Within a year he resigned from both posts, unable to cope with the political intrigue of the new Poland.

Paderewski returned to his first love, the concert stage, until he suffered a heart attack during an American tour in 1939. When Hitler invaded Poland later that year, Paderewski was appointed president of the Polish parliament in exile. He died two years later, while back in the United States raising money and support for his homeland.

The great patriot, composer, and musician was buried in Arlington National Cemetery in Washington, D.C. He requested that his heart be returned to Poland when his country became free once more.

*Besides being a great pianist and composer, Ignacy Jan Paderewski helped form the new Polish nation after World War I and served as its first premier.* (Courtesy Library of Congress)

# World War II

At dawn on September 1, 1939, Hitler's troops invaded Poland. Great Britain and France, who had pledged to defend Poland, declared war on Germany two days later. World War II had begun.

Once again, the Poles fought tenaciously against the invaders, but they proved no match for the all-powerful Nazi war machine. German planes and bombers obliterated the Polish air force in 48 hours. When German tanks rumbled across the countryside, they were met by a division of Polish cavalry armed with lances and sabers. Warsaw, the capital, surrendered on September 27, after 60,000 of its residents had been killed.

Ten days earlier, Soviet leader Joseph Stalin, who had signed a secret pact with Germany not to interfere with the Polish invasion, invaded Poland from the east. After a mere 21 years of independence, Poland was once again a conquered land.

The Germans divided their share of Poland into four districts, overseen by a Nazi governor-general who made his headquarters in Kraków. About a million Poles and Polish Jews were deported from their homes, and more than 700,000 Germans were sent to settle in their annexed lands.

The Russians made eastern Poland a part of Soviet Belorussia and the Ukraine. In August 1940 Stalin declared Lithuania, once a part of the Polish empire, a republic of the Soviet Union, which it remained for the next half-century.

Hitler's grand plan for Poland was a simple and brutal one. He would kill all the Jews, whom he blamed for Germany's problems, and reduce all other Poles to the status of slaves. To enact this plan he turned Poland into a killing ground. Concentration camps, vast prisons meant for the extermination of their inmates, were built in the once grassy countryside. Three of the most notorious Nazi death camps—Auschwitz, Treblinka, and Majdanek—were established in Poland, primarily so Poland's 3.5 million Jews would not have to be transported very far to be exterminated.

At first many non-Jewish Poles also went to the Nazi gas chambers, along with other Europeans and the Romany (Gypsies). This practice later stopped, and these non-Jewish Poles were put to work in the camps. A remarkable firsthand account of the gas chambers at Auschwitz is provided by Sophia Litwinska, a Polish prisoner:

> About half-past five in the evening [Christmas Day, 1941] trucks arrived and we were loaded into them, quite naked like animals, and were driven to the crematorium. . . . The whole truck was tipped over in the way they do it sometimes with potatoes or coal loads, and we were led into a room which gave me the impression of a shower-bath. There were towels hanging round, and sprays, and even mirrors. I cannot say how many were in the room altogether, because I was so terrified, nor do I know if the doors were

*The devastation wreaked on Poland during World War II is grimly captured in these two pictures of the old market in Warsaw before and after it was bombed.* (Courtesy Library of Congress)

closed. People were in tears; people were shouting at each other; people were hitting each other. . . . and suddenly I saw fumes coming in through a very small window at the top. I had to cough very

## MARIE CURIE (MANYA SKŁODOWSKA) (1867–1934)

She is perhaps the most distinguished Polish woman in modern times, but like so many of her 19th-century countrymen and women, she spent her entire career outside her war-torn homeland. Marie Curie received two Nobel Prizes for her scientific work, the first person to do so.

She was born Manya Skłodowska into a middle-class Warsaw family. Her father was a science professor, her mother, a musician. Manya could read at the age of four and graduated first in her class at 15. To pay her way through university she worked as a governess during the day and attended classes at night.

She studied math and science at the world-famous Sorbonne in Paris for a year. There she met the well-known scientist Pierre Curie, who had devised a law of magnetism, which was named for him. Curie fell in love with the intensely ambitious young woman, and they married in 1895. They became partners in work as well as in love and made a close study of radiation given off by the newly discovered radioactive substance uranium.

The Curies were confounded by the fact that uranium ore contained more radioactivity than the refined uranium. Where did the rest of it go? they asked themselves. They painstakingly extracted tiny amounts of radioactive elements from tons of uranium ore. The first new element they named polonium, in honor of Marie's homeland. The second element was discovered quite by accident.

When Marie returned to their ramshackle laboratory one evening in 1902, she saw a row of test tubes giving off an eerie bluish glow.

violently, tears were streaming from my eyes, and I had a sort of feeling in my throat as if I would be asphyxiated. I could not even look at the others because each of us concentrated on what happened to herself.

Incredibly, Litwinska was snatched from the gas chamber by Nazi guards and saved, because, she believed, she had come from a Lublin prison and had been sent there by mistake.

They called the substance radium. For their discovery of these elements the Curies shared the Nobel Prize in physics in 1903 with Antoine-Henri Becquerel, discoverer of natural radioactivity.

Pierre Curie died in a tragic street accident in 1906, and his wife took his place on the faculty at the Sorbonne, becoming the first woman to hold the position of teaching master. In 1911 she won her second Nobel Prize, in chemistry, for her work isolating radium. Three years later she helped found the Radium Institute, where she served as director.

During World War I, Marie Curie showed the beneficial use of radiation, helping to x-ray wounded soldiers at the front with her daughter Irene. This tireless scientist was still hard at work when she died in 1934. Her death was diagnosed as due to pernicious anemia caused by years of exposure to the substance she had spent much of her life studying—radium.

*Poland's greatest scientist, Marie Curie (Manya Skłodowska) won the Nobel Prize twice—once in physics and once in chemistry.* (Courtesy Library of Congress)

Among those Poles not sent to the camps were 2.5 million who were transported to Germany to work in labor camps. Another 200,000 Polish children were found to be "racially valuable" by the Nazis and sent to Germany to be what they called "Germanized"—trained to be good Germans.

Those Poles left in the occupied nation continued to resist. When the Germans took over Warsaw, they forced all remaining Jews into one section of the city and walled it off from the rest of Warsaw. In April

1943 the Nazis attempted to remove the 60,000 Jews left in the Warsaw Ghetto to concentration camps. The Jews resisted. Armed with only knives and stones, they fought their Nazi masters with a fierce and desperate will for a month. In the end 56,000 of them died. Those few thousands who survived were executed. A handful miraculously managed to escape and told the world of one of the war's most heroic episodes.

While underground activity and sabotage inside Poland went on, those Poles fortunate enough to have fled before and during the invasion joined the Allied efforts in France and Great Britain. A Polish army in exile was formed with 85,000 soldiers. When France fell to the Nazis, they fled to England. Poles continued to fight valiantly in the North African campaign and the Battle of Britain.

In June 1941 the Germans began a full assault on the Soviet Union, taking Stalin by surprise. The Russians now became part of the Allied cause, with the Nazis as their common enemy. The Russians were completely driven from Poland, which was now entirely in German hands.

But Hitler had taken on too many enemies. His army suffered its first major defeat in Russia and was forced to retreat. By mid-1944 the tide of war had turned dramatically. The Germans were losing, and the Poles took heart. In August the entire city of Warsaw rose up in rebellion. Their aim was twofold: to drive out the Nazis and keep the Russians from coming in. By now the Russians had begun to advance westward, liberating Polish territory from the Germans. They called themselves the Polish Committee of National Liberation (PCNL), the only legitimate power in Poland.

The Germans managed to hold the Russians back at the Vistula River and laid siege to Warsaw. An already-devastated city was reduced to rubble. The Germans bombed Warsaw from the air and on the ground. In two months they killed 200,000 people and leveled 90 percent of the buildings. The Soviets, who could have come to the aid of the Poles, had orders from their leader, Joseph Stalin, to wait outside the city and watch.

The extent of the suffering of the people of Warsaw can be glimpsed in this appeal written by Polish women to Pope Pius XII:

Most Holy Father . . . For three weeks, while defending our fortress, we have lacked food and medicines. Warsaw is in ruins. The Germans are killing the wounded in hospitals. They are making women and children march in front of them in order to protect their tanks. There is no exaggeration in reports of children who are fighting and destroying tanks with bottles of petrol [gasoline]. We mothers see our sons dying for freedom and the Fatherland. Holy Father, no-one is helping us. The Russian armies which have been for three weeks at the gates of Warsaw have not advanced a step. The aid coming to us from Great Britain is insufficient. The world is ignorant of our fight. God alone is with us. Holy Father, Vicar of Christ, if you can hear us, bless us Polish women who are fighting for the Church and for freedom.

Only when the Germans had done their worst did the Soviets move in and "liberate" what was left of Warsaw.

The wages of war were higher in Poland than in any other nation except for the Soviet Union. Six million Poles had died, half of them Jews. Of that total only 600,000—500,000 of them civilians—died in military confrontations. The nation's population had dropped by nearly a third of what it was at the war's start. Hundreds of towns were to be repopulated by Poles previously exiled to Russia and elsewhere. The Polish intelligentsia and Jewish population had been nearly exterminated. Other minorities had been uprooted by the war. What was left was a vast majority of Roman Catholic Poles.

# The Communist Era

Disillusioned by the failure of their government to prevent the slaughter, some Poles turned to communism as the best blueprint for Poland's future. This political doctrine called for a classless society in which workers shared in the products of their labor. The development of national communism in Poland fit in well with the plans of Stalin, who, like Hitler, dreamed of dominating Europe.

With the defeat of Germany and the end of the war, the Soviets were deeply entrenched in Poland, Czechoslovakia, Hungary, and much of the rest of Eastern Europe. The Soviet-controlled PCNL was running the Polish government, with Władysław Gomułka, leader of the communist Polish United Workers' Party (PZPR), as premier.

The Allies, pressured by the Polish national government in exile, agreed to recognize the Polish government if it included noncommunist political groups. The Soviets complied, but only for a while. By 1948 the Communist Party of Poland, supported by the Soviets, was in complete control of the country. To make their domination complete, the Soviets installed Konstantin Rokossovsky, a Russian military officer, as Polish minister of defense.

Those Polish Communist leaders who resisted Soviet influence were removed from power. Even Gomułka himself was forced to resign his post in 1948 and later put under house arrest. The following year a new constitution was adopted, a carbon copy of the Soviet constitution. Personal freedoms disappeared. Books and films were heavily censored. Agriculture and industry were taken out of the hands of individuals and controlled by the state.

But, just as they had resisted the Germans and countless invaders before them, the Poles defied the Communists. The Catholic Church, led by Stefan Cardinal Wyszyński (see boxed biography in chapter 5), was in the forefront of the resistance movement. In 1952 the cardinal began a three-year prison term, but the Poles continued to protest. In 1956 riots broke out in the ancient city of Poznań. Fifty thousand people marched in a demonstration, and a Communist security police officer was lynched. Soviet tanks were sent in to restore order, and more than 50 people were killed and 200 wounded.

A poem by Polish writer Adam Wazyk, published the previous year, expressed the anger and frustration of the Polish people under the yoke of communism. Here is an excerpt:

> there are exhausted people dying from heart attacks;
> there are people slandered and spat upon,
> people assaulted on the streets
> by common hoodlums, for whom legal definitions can't be
> found;
> there are people waiting for a scrap of paper;

*Stanisław Staszewski, a supporter of Władysław Gomułka, addresses a meeting shortly after Gomułka was restored to power in 1956.* (Courtesy Library of Congress)

> there are people waiting for justice;
> there are people who wait a long time.

Nikita Khrushchev, Stalin's more moderate successor in the Soviet Union, looked for a practical solution to the Polish problem. He wisely allowed Gomułka to return to power, realizing he was the only leader who could bring the people together. Khrushchev paid a visit to Warsaw in October 1956 and received Gomułka's assurance that he would not break off relations with the Soviet Union.

In what came to be called the Polish October, Gomułka instituted reforms in the rigid communist system to make it more acceptable to the people. Farmers were given back their land, and Polish Catholics were allowed to worship openly. Rokossovsky was removed from power and sent back to Russia. Cardinal Wyszyński was released from prison. Gomułka and Wyszyński worked out a pact of mutual cooperation. Life in communist Poland became somewhat better, but Poles continued to protest and demonstrate for more freedom into the 1960s.

By 1970 the situation had again worsened. When steep food price increases were announced on December 12, thousands of workers at the Lenin shipyard in Gdańsk, a hotbed of worker unrest, marched to party headquarters to protest. Two days later a general strike began. When demonstrators refused to disperse, police opened fire. Here is what happened as described by one shipyard striker who was there:

> One of the commanders, the lieutenant, just simply shot at the crowd with his pistol. It was about an arm's length from me, and I only realized what had happened when I saw this squirt of blood. One of the lads from the shipyard had been hit straight in the larynx, in the artery, and the blood—you know—it spouted up about four feet. It was oil on the flames, as we say in Polish: the people saw it, and they threw themselves at the police cordon. Then there was a massacre. . . .

The unrest quickly spread to other cities in the country. Gomułka was unable to control the situation and was replaced as Communist Party head by a likable ex-miner, Edward Gierek. Gierek tried to talk to the workers in their own language and reminded them that he had been a worker, too, and knew how they felt. Gaining a certain amount of cooperation from the workers, he made some positive reforms. He further improved relations with the church and forged stronger ties with noncommunist countries. But the economy, mismanaged by the Russians for two decades, continued to decline. Ordinary Poles could afford little more than the basics of life, and food prices soared higher and higher. Only when riots erupted in 1976 did the government put a halt to price increases.

Foreign loans, initiated by Gierek, had ended some of the country's pain, but by 1980 Poland was unable to pay back the loans and was deep in debt. Unrest grew throughout the land. Again it found its focal point in Gdańsk, where shipyard workers and others banded together to form a trade union. Their leader was a 37-year-old unemployed electrician named Lech Wałesa. They called their union movement Solidarity.

## NOTES

p. 17 "'By attacking Poland . . .'" *Encyclopedia Britannica,* vol. 18 (London: Encyclopaedia Britannica, 1965), p. 133.

pp. 17–18 "'We, the people of Poland . . .'" Norman Davies. *God's Playground*, vol. 2 (New York: Columbia University Press, 1982), p. 402.

p. 20 "'It is too late. . . .'" R. Kent Rasmussen. *The People's Almanac, No. 3* (New York: Bantam Books, 1981), p. 461.

p. 20 "'I came to speak to you . . .'" Carol Greene. *Poland* (Chicago: Children's Press, 1983), p. 107.

pp. 22–24 "'About half-past five in the evening . . .'" John Carey, ed. *Eyewitness to History* (New York: Avon, 1997), pp. 554–555.

p. 27 "'Most Holy Father . . .'" Davies, vol. 2, pp. 478–479.

pp. 28–29 "'there are exhausted people . . .'" Davies, vol. 2, p. 582.

p. 30 "'One of the commanders . . .'" Neal Ascherson. *The Struggles for Poland* (New York: Random House, 1987), p. 181.

# 3

# THE DOWNFALL OF COMMUNISM AND A FREE POLAND (1980 TO 2003)

Solidarity gave the Polish people an organization from which to build a national base of resistance to the Communists and a platform to get out their message. That message started as specific to the workers of 50 trade unions in Gdańsk, but under the skillful leadership of Lech Wałesa, an electrician turned union organizer, it soon spread to encompass all the grievances of the Polish people—political, economic, social, and spiritual.

## The Rise of Solidarity

During the long, hot summer of 1980 thousands of workers went on strike to protest the government's announcement that some meat prices would rise nearly 100 percent. "We must tell the people the truth regarding the disastrous situation of the country," wrote Mieczysław Rakowski, editor of *Polityka*, a weekly magazine. "A program of radical reform is urgently needed." From Warsaw to Lublin to Gdańsk the strikes spread.

The government had dealt with strikes before, but this was something else. Wałesa had organized millions of workers and supporters. The possibility of a general strike that could paralyze the entire nation was chillingly real.

## LECH WAŁESA (b. 1943)

One of modern Poland's great success stories, this son of a carpenter rose to become a leader in his people's struggle for freedom and went from being a jailed dissident to president of his nation in a few short years. Then, in as short a time Lech Wałesa went from being a national hero to a distrusted politician, whose popularity in one poll was lower than the man he helped overthrow, General Wojciech Jaruzelski. Whatever can be said about Wałesa, he stirs strong emotions in Poles, both for and against him.

He was born in Popaw during the Nazi occupation, one of eight children. On the death of his father, his mother married her brother-in-law and died in a traffic accident while visiting relatives in the

*Workers carry their leader, Lech Wałesa, on their shoulders in 1981 as they await a court ruling on the rights of farmers to form their own Solidarity-like union.* (AP Photo)

United States. The young Wałesa's stepfather decided to stay in America rather than return to communist Poland.

Wałesa went to state vocational school and later got a job as an electrician in Gdańsk's Lenin shipyard. When 55 shipyard workers died in the "bread riots" of December 1970, Wałesa's life was changed. He became a leading labor organizer, working to negotiate with the government for better working conditions and pay for the shipyard workers. In 1976 he was fired over a protest and spent years drifting from job to job trying to make a living for his family while continuing his work as a labor leader.

In January 1979 Wałesa cofounded a free trade union on the Baltic coast and helped publish the first issue of a radical journal, *The Worker of the Coast*. In August a strike among shipyard workers won Wałesa reinstatement as a worker. As the strike continued, Wałesa's demands included political rights as well as economic ones. On August 31, 1979, he signed the Gdańsk Agreement, giving workers in an Eastern bloc country, for the first time, the right to form unions and strike.

Placed under house arrest for 11 months during Poland's period of martial law, Wałesa emerged from this dark time apparently repentant, although not for long. In October 1982 he won the Nobel Peace Prize and became a figure of international fame. During the time of change in the Soviet Union in the mid-1980s, Wałesa's power and influence continued to grow, until he helped negotiate free elections with the Communists in 1989. In December 1990, his country now independent and the Communists out of power, Wałesa became the first freely elected president in Poland in more than 50 years.

Wałesa proved an embarrassment to many Poles, despite his heroic past. They were disturbed by his constant maneuvering to play kingmaker and cringed at his bad grammar. Others were angered by his expensive tastes at a time when many Poles were suffering severe economic hardships. At one point he moved into a renovated 17th-century palace, although the presidential residence was perfectly livable.

Wałesa lost the presidency in 1995 to Aleksander Kwaśniewski in a close election. In the 2000 election Wałesa attempted a political comeback but won only 1 percent of the vote. Although he has lost his popularity at home, Wałesa continues to be greatly admired abroad, especially in the United States, where he has visited and spoken many times.

On August 31 the government and the strikers came to an agreement in a Gdańsk conference hall. The government recognized the Gdańsk workers as a free and independent union with the right to strike. It promised workers better working conditions and health standards, less censorship, and Saturdays off. It even allowed workers to listen to radio broadcasts of Catholic Mass as they worked.

The idea of an organization of workers' unions was not unusual in the West, but in an Eastern bloc country in 1980, it was nothing less than revolutionary. No group of workers under Soviet communism had ever been able to form an independent union separate from the state.

Gierek, who had weathered many a political crisis in his 10 years in power, was seen as an ineffective leader by his Soviet masters and unable to deal with the unrest that led to the formation of Solidarity. In September 1980 he was forced to resign and was replaced by Stanisław Kania, a leading minister who had previously headed the army and the secret police.

A few weeks later the delegates of 36 independent unions from throughout Poland met in Gdańsk and united, calling themselves "Solidarity." When the organization attempted to legally register itself with a Warsaw court, the court delayed the action. It later asked the union to recognize the Communist Party and its "leading role" in Poland. Solidarity refused and gave the government until November 12 to recognize it or face a general strike. Two days before the deadline the government backed down and granted Solidarity its charter without the language change. It was the first time a labor organization independent of the Communist Party had been recognized in a communist country.

If the government thought it could contain Solidarity by legitimatizing it, it was mistaken. On December 14, 1980, a thousand farmers gathered in Warsaw to form their own power base. They founded Rural Solidarity, demanding the same rights and privileges as the industrial workers of Solidarity. When the government held up the registration of the new organization, the farmers staged a sit-in in the city of Rzeszów that lasted into February. When Solidarity came to the support of the farmers, the government agreed to negotiate. Although recognition did not come, Rural Solidarity held its first congress in Poznań in west-central Poland in March 1981. The same month the police broke up a sit-in of Rural Solidarity members in Bydgoszcz, about 50 miles northeast of Poznań, and three people were seriously injured. Solidarity threatened a nationwide strike unless the guilty parties were punished. Soon after, Rural Solidarity was officially recognized by the government.

To illustrate how far the government had sunk, in a June poll the top three most respected institutions in Poland were the Catholic Church, Solidarity, and the army. The Communist Party ranked 14th. When the first anniversary of the Gdańsk accords arrived, Solidarity's membership numbered 10 million.

In September, Solidarity's first National Congress of Delegates convened in Gdańsk with the celebration of Mass by Archbishop Józef Glemp, the newly named primate of Poland. Glemp succeeded Cardinal Wyszyński who had died in May. When the first session of the congress ended with a letter of support to workers in the Soviet Union and Eastern Europe, the Soviets branded the congress "an anti-Socialist and anti-Soviet orgy." The danger of Solidarity's fever of freedom spreading was now seen as an imminent threat to the Communists.

The Polish government faced a serious dilemma. If it gave in any more to the unions, it could jeopardize the future of the state and provide a model for the peoples of other Eastern bloc countries to imitate. In October, Kania was replaced by the prime minister, General Wojciech Jaruzelski, a man the Soviets felt was moderate enough to deal effectively with Solidarity without giving away any more power.

## Martial Law

In an unheard-of move, Wałesa, Jaruzelski, and Archbishop Glemp had a summit meeting to talk about how they might work together to bring Poland out of its crisis. However, further talks made little headway as the economy grew grimmer and grimmer. Economic figures released in November showed industrial production down 15 percent from the previous year. Solidarity's leadership supported the call from its Warsaw chapter for a nationwide day of protest on December 17, 1981, but the protest never took place.

During the night of December 12, Polish troops, under orders from General Jaruzelski, sealed off Poland's cities. All telephone and telegraph lines within the country were cut. The leaders of Solidarity, in Gdańsk for a national meeting, were rounded up by police and arrested.

On a sunny Sunday morning, Poles woke up to their darkest day since the communist takeover in 1948. Martial law had been declared by General Jaruzelski. All public gatherings were banned, all civil rights suspended, a 10:00 P.M. to 6:00 A.M. curfew was declared, all schools were closed, and more than 10,000 people, including Wałesa, were detained or imprisoned.

The suddenness of the government's action caught the people off guard. The sight of tanks in the streets reminded many Poles of the grim days of World War II. Strikes and demonstrations continued, but now they were met with bloody reprisals from the police and army. The Polish ambassador to the United States, Romuald Spasowski, stated that "the cruel night of darkness and silence has spread over my country" and defected to the United States.

Gradually Poland's borders were reopened and communications reestablished, but "temporary" martial law continued for nearly a year. In October 1982, Jaruzelski officially outlawed Solidarity. Only a few brave members of parliament opposed the motion, including future prime minister Hanna Suchocka.

Jaruzelski released some of the union leaders, and by 1984 they had all been released. He hoped they had learned their lesson and would not attempt to threaten the state's authority again. But the government's actions had only increased the determination of the leaders of Solidarity to continue the struggle for political and economic freedom.

The movement received two boosts in its efforts from abroad. In October 1982, the very month that Solidarity was outlawed, Wałesa won the Nobel Peace Prize. In acknowledging Wałesa's peaceful efforts to bring about democratic change in his country, the world put further pressure on the Polish government to reform itself. Then in June 1983 John Paul II visited his homeland for the third time since becoming pope. A fervent advocate for Polish freedom since his days as a priest, the pope met with both Jaruzelski and Wałesa and worked as a mediator between the two. With Solidarity outlawed, the church in Poland had taken over the role of the nation's conscience and called repeatedly for the full reinstatement of civil rights.

Jaruzelski may have banned Solidarity, but he could not ban the yearning for freedom it had stirred in the hearts of the Polish people.

Demonstrations soon began again, with the firm support of the Catholic Church.

In October 1984 a heinous crime brought the Polish people to their feet in protest. Father Jerzy Popieluszko, a young radical priest in north Warsaw and a strong supporter of Solidarity, was abducted and murdered by a gang of secret police. Jaruzelski denied that his government was responsible for the murder and put the killers on public trial. The murderers claimed they had been encouraged by senior officials, although no one else was charged in the case. Half a million Poles poured into Warsaw to attend the funeral of the martyred priest. "Rest in peace," Wałesa said at the funeral. "Solidarity is alive, because you have given your life for it."

Then change in the Soviet Union made change in Poland all but inevitable. In 1985 Mikhail Gorbachev came to power in Moscow and began a series of reforms to open up Soviet society, end corruption, and promote economic growth. To improve the economy Gorbachev made sharp cuts in military spending and loosened the stranglehold the Soviets had on their Eastern bloc neighbors. As the Soviet Union focused on improving life at home, it pulled back its influence in these other communist countries. This only further served to undercut the authority of the government in Poland and gave Jaruzelski, who argued his actions were only meant to prevent a Soviet invasion of Poland, room to negotiate with Solidarity.

## The First Free Elections

In early 1989, thanks to the efforts of Solidarity and the earth-shattering changes in the Soviet Union, the unthinkable happened. President Jaruzelski agreed to sit down at the bargaining table with Solidarity. A series of roundtable talks began. Wałesa pressed the government to agree to the holding of free and open elections in which Solidarity candidates could run against those put forth by the Communist Party. In April 1989 the two sides signed accords that once again made Solidarity legal and paved the way for the first free elections in Poland since World War II. The people would vote for delegates to serve in a two-house parliament and a president to be elected for a six-year term. The agreement would give the Communists 38 percent of all parliamentary seats in the lower house and 35 percent to members of Solidarity. The remaining 27 percent of the delegates would come from numerous smaller political parties. There would be no quotas for the upper house, or Senate. All 100 seats were up for grabs, and Solidarity hoped to get a majority of them.

Wałesa emerged from the negotiations as a major power to be reckoned with. "[F]or the first time we have talked to each other using the force of arguments, and not arguments of force," he said. "It bids well for the future, I believe, that the roundtable discussions can become the beginning of the road for democracy and a free Poland."

Surprisingly Wałesa himself did not run as a candidate in the elections scheduled for June 1989. He preferred to coordinate activities behind the scenes, although he expressed interest in running for president in 1995.

As the elections drew closer, the Communists found themselves, for the first time in their lives, having to compete for votes with other political parties. Many Communists claimed they were not opposed to reform. Even Jaruzelski himself now seemed to welcome it. Like Gorbachev, however, he hoped to keep it within the scheme of a communist system of government.

"The majority [of Communists] are in the middle, and they are waiting to see whether the reforms will succeed," said Liberal Party member Ludwick Kusecki. "If they succeed they will be with us. . . ."

June 4, election day in Poland, was anticipated with hope around the world. Poland was the first of the Eastern bloc countries to move toward democracy, and it was not expected to be the last. The government of Hungary was also inching toward reform. And while the Communists held tenaciously onto East Germany, Czechoslovakia, Romania, and Bulgaria, the people of these countries looked hopefully to Poland.

When the voting was over, Solidarity had won a resounding victory. While the Communists, as predicted, held a majority in the lower house, Solidarity delegates swept into the Senate, taking 99 of the 100 seats. The Communists were further embarrassed by the results of some elections in which party candidates ran unopposed but still failed to get the 50 percent of the vote needed to win. Jaruzelski squeezed into office as the new president by one vote in parliament. Many Solidarity members abstained, refusing to vote for a former Communist adversary.

July 4, 1989, was a historic day in Poland as Solidarity delegates marched proudly into the parliament building. They had come from being outlaws in their country to being its legitimate lawmakers. How they would use their newfound power was a matter of intense debate. Some wanted to make the Communists pay for the 40 years of misery they had inflicted on Poland. More moderate members wanted to work with the Communists and gain their support in facing the daunting challenges of political and economic reform that lay ahead.

Jaruzelski was ready to negotiate. On July 25 he met for two hours with Wałesa, but the Solidarity leader rejected his offer of a coalition. Why, Wałesa reasoned, should he join up with the Communists when Solidarity was now "those forces that enjoyed the support of a majority of society."

Jaruzelski, who had pledged in his role as president of a new Poland to resign as Communist Party head, was replaced by the country's prime minister, Mieczysław Rakowski. The new prime minister who replaced Rakowski was a man despised by many Poles. Czesław Kiszczak had been interior minister in the early 1980s and supervised the establishment of martial law and the arrest of many Solidarity leaders. Within two weeks Kiszczak resigned under pressure, and Solidarity organizer Tadeusz Mazowiecki, a Catholic lawyer and journalist, became the first noncommunist head of an Eastern bloc government since the end of World War II. "I think we can gather our strength from within ourselves," Mazowiecki said soon after taking power. "This is not easy, but it is possible if everyone begins to realize and to feel that we are now on our own, and that it all has some sense and can lead somewhere."

In November Wałesa went to the United States, where he addressed a joint meeting of Congress. Wałesa made an impassioned plea for foreign aid, aid that would be desperately needed if Poland were to change from a communist economy to a free-market one.

We have heard many beautiful words of encouragement. These are appreciated, but being a worker and a man of concrete work, I must tell you that the supply of words on the world market is plentiful but the demand is falling. Let deeds follow words now . . . It is now worth recalling this great American plan which helped Western Europe to protect its freedom and peaceful order [the Marshall Plan]. And now

it is the moment when Eastern Europe awaits an investment of this
kind—an investment in freedom, democracy, and peace, an investment adequate to the greatness of the American nation.

# The Downfall of Communism and the Division of Solidarity

As Poles increased their own investment in their new, bright future, it
became increasingly apparent that the Communist Party would not be
part of that future. Under more and more pressure from the people and
their representatives in the new parliament, the Communist Party of
Poland voted to disband itself on January 28, 1990. At about the same
time, the government, led by Prime Minister Mazowiecki, declared a program of radical economic reform that would move Poland from the poorly
planned economy of the Communists to a free-market economy such as
in the Western democracies. On January 1, 1990, price controls were
lifted and prices of food and other products skyrocketed. Bread rose an
average of 40 percent in one week. Electricity rose 400 percent and coal
600 percent. A tank of gas cost more than many Poles earned in a week.

At the same time, state enterprises were "privatized," sold off to private individuals or groups, and subsidies, or financial assistance, to government businesses were abruptly ended. These businesses were pushed
into bankruptcy, and workers were paid unemployment compensation
until they could find new jobs. Jeffrey Sachs, the Harvard professor hired
as a consultant by the new government, called this approach to changing
the economy "shock therapy."

By September another major shock wave swept the halls of government. Jaruzelski, the man who saw the June election as "a huge step
toward democracy," was pushed out by that same democratic movement.
He resigned from his office, and new presidential elections were set for
the end of the year.

But if communism had crumbled, the movement that had brought
about its end was splintering. Solidarity no longer reflected the meaning
of that word. With the goal of independence achieved and communism
dead, there was no common enemy to fight. As Wałesa himself pointed

out before the election, "What was needed were politicians, not dissidents, and politics has to do largely with compromise." But compromise was not easy to find among the dozens of political parties that had sprung up in the wake of communism. The diversity of opinion was admirable, but it stymied any kind of consensus for the future of the new nation.

Prime Minister Mazowiecki found his chief rival in the December 1990 election for president was none other than Lech Wałesa himself. The two men now stood on opposing sides. Mazowiecki, the first intellectual to support Solidarity, represented the politicians and technocrats, and Wałesa, the man of the common people, stood for labor and the more conservative Catholic section of the organization. Wałesa won the election and was sworn into office on December 22, 1990. It was the first completely free election in Poland in more than half a century, and Wałesa was the first popularly elected president in that time.

Poland's struggle for freedom was finally over, but the new challenges of changing over to a democracy, politically and economically, were just beginning. Wałesa's choice for prime minister, Jan Krzysztof Bielecki, kept the economic reforms moving full steam ahead. The privatization of state businesses forged forward, and more than a million new jobs were created in the private sector. But the downfall of the communist economy put millions of other Poles out of work. For the first time in decades Poland faced a serious unemployment problem. Shock therapy was shocking the people out of their complacency, and hope was being replaced by fear of an unknown future in the brave new world of a free-market economy.

# The Democratic Union versus the Democratic Left Alliance

When the first fully free parliamentary elections were held in October 1991, voter turnout was only 42 percent. The parliament they elected was a fractured and fragmented body representing 29 political parties. Wałesa appointed a coalition government, but without support in the parliament it fell apart by June 1992. The president tried to put another prime minister, Waldemar Pawlak (b. 1959), head of the Polish Peasant Party, into office but failed to get enough support for him. Instead, Hanna Suchocka, head of the Democratic Union Party, was chosen as a compromise candidate who was popular with all sectors of the parliament. She became the first female prime minister in eastern Europe in the 20th century.

A longtime dissident against the Communists, Suchocka proved her commitment to economic reform by keeping the shock therapy in place. She also showed she had the backbone needed to run the country by standing up to striking workers in May 1992. But economic reforms continued to raise unemployment and create misery. Suchocka's coalition alliance with the church, which under communism would have been admired, was now bringing sharp criticism. The church's paternal role in Polish life, especially in politics, was less acceptable in a free Poland than it had been under communism. The government backed the church ban against abortion with legislation and earned the resentment of millions of Poles.

As the Democratic Union came under attack, the former Communists regrouped. They now called themselves the Democratic Left Alliance (SLD) and put themselves forward as a viable alternative to the shock therapy of the reformers. They promised change, too, but at a slower pace that would not cause undue hardship to the common people.

Surprising as it seemed, the once-reviled Communists now appeared to be a comforting link with the past for many Poles. "The former Communists are the only ones who can really make order out of this mess," said Jan Binkowski, a former baker. "They have experience. In the forty years when we had Communism, we did rebuild, we did achieve something. In the past four years, we've driven unemployment up to four million, closed a lot of state enterprises and ruined a lot."

One of the people held most responsible for Poland's problems was the former champion of Solidarity, Wałesa. His failure to form a workable government was blamed largely on his own thirst for power and desire for control.

"He's like a commemorative statue," declared worker Henryk Grosiask. "When it's first welded and shining, people come to see it but after a while it stops shining and people stop coming."

Another observer, sociologist Wojciek Pawlak, summed up Wałesa's fatal flaw more perceptively: "His strength is turning people against something or someone. He can't very well turn the people against himself now that he is the highest public official."

But in September 1993, when the election results were in, that appeared to be exactly what Wałesa and his new "nonparty movement for reform" did. The SLD took 20 percent of the vote; the Polish Peasant Party (PSL), a socialist-leaning group, gained 16 percent; the Democratic Union came in third with about 10 percent; and Wałesa's Nonparty Bloc took a meager 5 percent. The people had spoken.

SLD leader Aleksander Kwaśniewski, a junior minister in the Communist government during the 1980s, was expected to become the new prime minister, but the job went instead to Waldemar Pawlak. Pawlak's Polish Peasant Party formed a coalition with the Alliance. "I want the material well-being to be revealed not in statistics," Pawlak told the nation, "but in every Polish home." This was the kind of language the people understood.

Poland had led the way toward freedom in eastern Europe in 1989. Now, four years later, it was leading the way back toward the familiar. Former Communists were also beginning a comeback in Hungary, Bulgaria, and Romania.

Perhaps the most startling aspect of the Communist comeback was not that so many Poles wanted it, but that few of them had any fear of what it might lead to. As President Wałesa said after the election, "Nothing can happen because we have democracy, a free press, magnificent youth. . . ."

# A New Government

But Wałesa's optimism was soon shattered. In the presidential election of November 1995, he was challenged by Kwaśniewski. Nine years younger than Wałesa, Kwaśniewski ran a vibrant, pragmatic campaign, making economic reform his central issue. Wałesa was arrogant and aloof and in a televised debate with Kwaśniewski even refused to shake his opponent's hand. His rude behavior lost him the goodwill of many who had supported him in the past. Even more damning was his poor record of achievement as president.

On election day, Kwaśniewski narrowly defeated Wałesa by a 3 percent margin. "Mr. Kwaśniewski's victory," wrote Radek Sikorski in the *Wall Street Journal Europe*, "marks the end of what might be called the

## JOLANTA KWAŚNIEWSKA (b. 1955)

She has been described as a cross between U.S. first ladies Jacqueline Kennedy and Hillary Clinton. Poles respect her husband, President Aleksander Kwaśniewski, but it is Jolanta Kwaśniewska whom they truly love. She is Poland's "first First Lady."

She was born in Gdańsk on June 3, 1955, and met Kwaśniewski while studying law at University of Gdańsk. She graduated, became a lawyer, and married Kwaśniewski in 1979. The couple had a daughter Aleksandra, two years later.

Kwaśniewska established her own real estate business in 1991. When her husband was elected president of Poland in 1995, he gave it up to pursue a busy schedule as first lady. Among the many charitable causes she has raised money for are poor and disabled children, AIDS patients, orphans, and breast cancer awareness. Her foundation, Communications without Barriers, has created a medical center for children in need of bone marrow transplants.

But it is not just her good works that have made Kwaśniewska the most popular and admired woman in Poland today. She is extremely attractive, well educated, athletic, and stylish. No previous wife of a Polish politician has been so admired by the public and has spent so much time in the spotlight. She has accompanied her husband on many state visits, including trips to the United States and the United Kingdom.

Kwaśniewska has been called "a post-feminist First Lady," who is subordinate in some ways, but very independent in others. She is a devout Roman Catholic, while her husband, a former Communist, is an

heroic era of Polish politics. For the former dissidents who dominated Polish politics since Communism's collapse in 1989, the election result is not just a political reversal but a judgement on their entire lives."

Kwaśniewski quickly proved a popular president, but his personal popularity could not help his party, which was unable to reverse many of the growing economic problems left over from the Wałesa years. As the two largest political parties, Solidarity and the SLD, became more moderate, their sharpest differences began to fade. One political observer compared them to the two political parties in the United States, with Solidarity

atheist. Despite her faith, she has publicly opposed the prohibition of the medical procedure amniocentesis, a prenatal diagnostic test that the Catholic Church is against.

When asked about her many activities, Kwaśniewska has said, "I only have one child and I am full of energy. I hate when I have nothing to do, it would kill me."

*Polish first lady Jolanta Kwaśniewska (right) walks arm in arm with U.S. first lady Laura Bush at the Pennsylvania Academy of the Arts in Philadelphia during a state visit in July 2002.* (AP Photo/Dan Loh)

reflecting the values of the Democrats and the SLD, of the Republicans. The post-election SLD lost support among workers for its growing alignment with big business and the bureaucratic civil service, so much a part of the old communist system. In the 1997 parliamentary elections Solidarity won a significant victory with 34 percent of the popular vote, compared to SLD's 27 percent. A third political party, the Freedom Union (UW), made up mostly of intellectuals, professionals, and former dissidents, won 13 percent of the vote. Solidarity and UW formed a coalition government.

# Joining the European Community

In 1999, Poland, along with the Czech Republic and Hungary, was admitted as a full member of the North Atlantic Treaty Organization (NATO). It was a triumphant moment for Poles of all political persuasions, who felt they had finally achieved their goal of being fully accepted by the West. Poland's neighbor Russia, on the other hand, was not happy about the new alliance but accepted it. And not all Poles were as enthusiastic about Poland's attempts to join the European Union (EU), an organization of 15 European nations who trade with one another.

Farmers' Union leader Andrzej Lepper, for example, was an outspoken critic of government policies toward Poland's small farmers and believed joining the EU would further undermine them. "The EU is not interested in helping Poland," he declared. "The EU is only interested in helping itself and making Poland a good market for its products." Those products, he believed, would hurt the Polish farmer, who would be undersold by foreign goods. In early 1999, under Lepper's direction, 20,000 Polish farmers blocked 100 roadways in protest. Government negotiations ended the protest, but ill feelings among the farmers and farmworkers continued.

# The 2000 Elections and a New Prime Minister

President Kwaśniewski enjoyed an overwhelming victory in the presidential election of 2000, winning nearly 54 percent of the popular vote. He became the first Polish president in history to win reelection. The election also sounded the death knell of Wałesa's political career: He won only 1 percent of the vote. The following year Kwaśniewski appointed Leszek Miller, chairman of the SLD, as the new prime minister. A seasoned politician who held several ministerial positions through the 1990s, Miller worked closely with Kwaśniewski to improve the economy and stabilize the country.

But at the beginning of the 21st century, problems continued. Poland became a victim of the slowing global economy, unemployment hit a new high of 17 percent, and dissatisfaction among the large working class increased. Lepper's legitimacy as a spokesman for the disenfranchised was damaged by charges of demagoguery. He was censured by the government in 2002 and charged with slander.

But there was an even more serious threat to the government—from within. The Polish Peasant Party (PSL) formed part of the three-way coalition government with the SLD and the Union of Labor (UP). However, the PSL opposed Poland's entry into the EU and refused to cooperate on major legislature unless a bill it backed was passed. "It is impossible to be in the government and oppose it at the same time," said Prime Minister Miller in a speech to the nation. "I am not and will not be anybody's hostage." Miller backed his words with action and dropped the PSL from the government coalition. The move, however, left the government more vulnerable than ever: It no longer commanded a majority in parliament and would have to seek other political partners to push through its legislative programs.

Despite these setbacks, Poland remains well along the road to democracy and a free-market economy. Some of the problems it faces are the same that beset many Western democracies. Unlike a number of its neighbors, including Russia, Poland's future is relatively bright and secure. It has the tools and the will to continue to forge a nation that meets the needs of all its people. It must now push forward to that worthy goal with determination and an unyielding spirit.

## NOTES
p. 33 "'We must tell the people . . .'" Lawrence Weschler. *Solidarity: Poland in the Season of Its Passion* (New York: Simon & Schuster, 1982), p. 169.

p. 37 "'an anti-Socialist and anti-Soviet orgy.'" Weschler, p. 191.

p. 38 "'the cruel night of darkness . . .'" Romuald Spasowski. *The Liberation of One.* (San Diego, Calif.: Harcourt Brace Jovanovich, 1986), p. 7.

p. 39 "'Rest in peace. . . .'" Neal Ascherson. *The Struggles for Poland* (New York: Random House, 1987), p. 227.

p. 40 "'[F]or the first time . . .'" Bernard Gwertzman and Michael T. Kaufman, eds. *The Collapse of Communism* (New York: Times Books, 1990), p. 35.

p. 40 "'The majority [of Communists] . . .'" Gwertzman and Kaufman, p. 113.

p. 41 "'those forces that enjoyed . . .'" Gwertzman and Kaufman, p. 126.

p. 41 "'I think we can . . .'" Gwertzman and Kaufman, p. 130.

pp. 41–42 "'We have heard many beautiful words . . .'" Gwertzman and Kaufman, pp. 207–208.

p. 43 "'What was needed were politicians . . .'" Gwertzman and Kaufman, p. 36.

p. 44 "'The former Communists are the only ones . . .'" *New York Times*, September 12, 1993, p. 14.

p. 44 "'He's like a commemorative statue. . . .'" *New York Times*, September 19, 1993, p. 3.

p. 44 "'His strength is turning people against . . .'" *New York Times*, September 19, 1993, p. 3.

p. 45 "'I want the material well-being . . .'" *New York Times*, October 28, 1993, p. A6.

p. 45 "'Nothing can happen . . .'" *New York Times*, September 25, 1993, n.p.

p. 45 "Mr. 'Kwaśniewski's victory marks the end . . .'" Radek Sikorski, *Wall Street Journal Europe*, November 21, 1995, p. A14.

pp. 46–47 "'a post-feminist First Lady'" and "'I only have one child . . .'" *New York Times*, June 11, 1999, p. A4.

p. 48 "'The EU is not interested in helping Poland . . .'" *New York Times*, November 30, 2001, p. A14.

p. 49 "'It is impossible to be in government . . .'" Witold Zygulski. *Warsaw Voice*. Available on-line. URL: http://www.warsawvoice.pl/. Downloaded March 12, 2003.

# PART II
# Poland Today

# 4

# GOVERNMENT

Under communism the Polish government was run by 7 percent of the people, those Poles who belonged to the Polish United Workers' Party, or the Communist Party of Poland. The one-house legislature consisted of 460 members, the vast majority of them party members. When the Sejm was not in session, 17 of its members, forming the Council of State, ran the government. A prime minister, eight deputy prime ministers, and 20 ministers who ran government departments, composed the Council of Ministers, appointed by the Sejm. In effect, the Polish People's Republic was a republic in name only. It was run by a small hierarchy within the Communist Party.

## The Three Branches of Government

At present some of these same Communists are back in power, but the structure of the government they run is radically different from what it was under communism. The first free elections, held in June 1989, created a new legislative body made up of two houses—an upper house, the Senat (Senate), consisting of 100 members, and a lower house, the Sejm, made up of 460 members as in the previous government. In the first election the Communists were guaranteed a certain number of seats in the Sejm, but that changed in the next election, held in July 1990.

A revised constitution in June 1990 called for a new executive branch—a president to be elected by the people. The president's role, however, unlike in the United States, is subordinate to that of the prime minister, who actually runs the government with his ministers. The president appoints the prime minister, although his choice is subject to the approval of the parliament. The president is also involved in foreign policy and has veto power over legislation proposed by parliament. His veto can be overturned by a two-thirds majority of parliament.

On the local level, government is run by councils that are elected every four years. The country is divided into 16 provinces called voivodships, or in Polish, *wojewodztwo*. These voivodships are divided into 822 towns and 2,121 wards, or *gmina*. The councils run local serv-

*The new complex of parliamentary buildings, shown here, was built on the site of the original Parliament building, which was reduced to rubble during World War II.* (Courtesy Polish National Tourist Office)

ices with money from a combination of local and central government taxes. District agencies help link local councils with the central government.

The third branch of government, the judiciary, is headed by the Supreme Court in Warsaw that hears final appeals on cases and oversees the legal system. Under that is an administrative supreme court and a court of appeals. Under communism there were no jury trials in Poland; all decisions were made by judges, appointed for five-year terms. District courts handle most civil and criminal cases. County or provincial courts handle more serious or important cases. There are also 65 family consultative centers, set up in 1977, to handle domestic relations and divorce. Ordinary courts began to handle divorce cases, which are on the rise in Poland, in 1990. District court judges are elected, while Supreme Court judges are appointed by the president from candidates proposed by the National Council of the Judiciary. The Constitutional Tribunal is a special body that interprets the laws of the Constitution of 1997 and hears constitutional complaints from ordinary citizens.

# A Popular President

Aleksander Kwaśniewski, despite his Communist past, has proven to be a popular and effective leader. Born in Białogard in northwestern Poland on November 15, 1954, he studied economics at the University of Gdańsk, where he was also an athlete. He joined the Polish United Workers' Party (PZPR) in 1977 and was editor of two youth magazines in the early 1980s, one of them the first Polish computer magazine, which he also founded. After the PZPR dissolved in 1990, Kwaśniewski cofounded the Democratic Left Alliance (SLD) the following year.

As president, Kwaśniewski has helped Poland gain international stature. Fluent in English, German, and Russian, he has been an effective advocate of his country to both the United States and Russia. In January 2002 he welcomed to Poland President Vladimir Putin, the first Russian leader to visit the country in nearly a decade. The meeting helped repair damage in Polish-Russian relations and promote goodwill. The two presidents signed several trade accords, something Poland needs to help pay

*Polish president Aleksander Kwaśniewski (left) and U.S. president George W. Bush. Under Kwaśniewski's leadership, Poland has become one of the United States's strongest allies in Europe.* (Courtesy Embassy of the Republic of Poland, Washington, D.C.)

off its $4.5 billion debt to Russia.

U.S. president George W. Bush visited Poland as Kwaśniewski's guest in June 2001. Kwaśniewski at that time voiced his support for Bush's controversial plan to build an antimissile shield, which some NATO members have said is in violation of an old U.S.-Russian treaty from 1972.

In July 2002 Kwaśniewski visited the United States at President Bush's invitation. The visit strengthened Polish-American ties. Kwaśniewski gave Bush his commitment of military support in keeping post-Taliban Afghanistan stable and secure. For his part, Bush promised more economic aid and help in strengthening the Polish military.

"Poland," Bush said in a speech during Kwaśniewski's visit, "is an example to all of Europe. After all, it's a strong democracy with a market economy, a nation prepared to play an influential role on the world stage."

# Foreign Relations

At the start of the 21st century, Poland has continued to grow closer in its relations with the West, particularly the United States. When the United States went to war against Iraq to end the dictatorship of Saddam Hussein, in March 2003, Poland was, after Great Britain, the United States's staunchest ally in Europe. Two hundred Polish soldiers fought as part of the coalition forces in Iraq, including 56 members of Poland's Special Forces unit.

The following month Poland signed an agreement to buy 48 U.S.-made F-16 jet fighters for $3.5 billion. It was the largest defense contract by a former member of the Soviet bloc since the cold war had ended. The jets, to arrive in 2006, will upgrade the Polish air force to meet NATO requirements. The two nations further agreed for the United States to make technology and economic investments in Poland valued up to $12 billion.

At the same time Poland has not neglected its ties with neighboring Russia. Polish foreign minister Włodzimierz Cimoszewicz visited Moscow in February 2003. He met with the Committee for Russian-Polish Cooperative Strategy to discuss the delivery of Russian natural gas to Poland and in return Polish goods to Russia, which will help to reduce a trade deficit. Beginning in July 2003 Russians can obtain Polish visas to freely travel there.

Placing itself between the West and the East, Poland is putting itself in position to benefit from both sides and make itself one of the most important countries in Europe.

**NOTE**

p. 56 "'Poland is an example to all of Europe. . . .'" *New York Times*, July 19, 2002, p. A13.

**GROWTH OF POLAND**

SWEDEN

*Baltic Sea*

TEUTONIC KNIGHTS

Novgorod

RUSSIAN PRINCIPALITIES

*Volga R.*

Danzig

Vilna

*Western Divina R.*

Smolensk

Moscow

*Oka R.*

Minsk

*Vistula R.*

Warsaw

POLAND-LITHUANIA

Kursk

*Don R.*

*Oder R.*

HOLY
ROMAN
EMPIRE

Kraków

Kiev

*Dnieper R.*

CRIMEAN
KHANATE

HUNGARY

*Dniester R.*

*Bug R.*

*Donets R.*

*Prut R.*

MOLDAVIA

*Don R.*

OTTOMAN EMPIRE

*Black Sea*

–·–·–  Poland in 1386, at time of union with Lithuania

– – – – –  Lithuania in 1386, at time of union with Poland

Territorial gains by 1470, on the eve of
Poland-Lithuania's gradual reduction in the
east by an expansionist Principality of Moscow

# 5

# RELIGION

To say that Poland is a Catholic country is about as much of an under-
statement as saying the pope is Catholic. (The pope is also Polish.)
Roughly 95 percent of the population is Roman Catholic. The Polish
people, particularly in the villages and rural areas, are among the most
devoutly religious Catholics in the world.

In 1978 Polish Catholicism took on a new meaning for the world.
Karol Cardinal Wojtyla, archbishop of Kraków, was elected pope of the
Roman Catholic Church. As John Paul II, he became the first non-
Italian pope in more than 450 years and the first Polish pope ever. Even
more important, John Paul II was the first pope from a communist coun-
try, and the effect that had in Eastern Europe, and particularly in
Poland, was extraordinary.

A year after becoming pope, John Paul visited his homeland and
called on the Communist government to allow more freedom to the people. This speech inspired millions of Poles to resist the Communists and
gave particular hope and courage to one man—Lech Wałesa, leader of
the labor group Solidarity.

Catholicism was first introduced in Poland in A.D. 966. Since then
the church has become an integral part of Polish society and culture
and has been called the very soul of the Polish people. It was the
church that gave Poles the support and faith to withstand endless
hoards of invaders from the Mongols to the Soviet Communists. When

## STEFAN CARDINAL WYSZYŃSKI (1901–1981)

If the Catholic Church is the soul of the Polish people, the soul of the church for three decades was Cardinal Wyszyński. This beloved head of the Polish church defended his faith from the Communists, learned to accommodate them to survive, and lived to see the rebirth of new hope for his people with the coming of Solidarity.

Wyszyński was born in the village of Zuzela in Russian-occupied Poland. He was ordained a priest on his 23rd birthday and became vicar of the basilica at Włoclawek. Wyszyński 's commitment to social causes as well as religious ones became quickly evident. He earned a doctorate in sociology and canon law at the Catholic University at Lublin. For a time he edited a Catholic daily newspaper and wrote several books about labor issues.

When World War II broke out, the fearless priest worked against the Nazis in the Warsaw underground. In 1946, a year after the war's end, he was made bishop of Lublin. Three years later Wyszyński rose to the highest office of the church, primate of Poland, at the very moment the Communists were taking over his country.

Although Wyszyński made an uneasy alliance with the Communists, he knew they would do everything to break his power and that of the church. When he was elected a cardinal in November 1952, he refused to go to the Vatican to be consecrated, fearing he might not be allowed back into Poland. The following year he was arrested at home by the secret police. When his faithful dog bit the hand of one of the arresting officers, the cardinal carefully bandaged the wound

Poland ceased to exist as a country at the end of the 18th century, the church sustained the people and gave them hope when all hope seemed lost. " . . . the history of the Roman Catholic Church provides one of the very few threads of continuity in Poland's past," writes historian Norman Davies. "Kingdoms, dynasties, republics, parties, and regimes have come and gone; but the Church seems to go on forever."

Unlike previous conquerors of Poland, the Communists were atheists who opposed religion. In their first eight years in power they did

before being taken away. He spent three years in prison without ever coming to trial.

In 1956 one of the first acts of the new prime minister, Władysław Gomułka, was to release Wyszyński from prison. The pragmatic Communist and the equally practical cardinal formed a long-lasting pact of cooperation. Gomułka gave the church more freedom than it enjoyed in any other Soviet bloc country, and the cardinal supported the "national communism" of Gomułka's government.

For all his compromising, Wyszyński remained a staunch defender of the faith and resisted the new Communist leadership when Gomułka was replaced in 1970. A decade

The leader of the Catholic Church in Poland during some of its darkest days, Cardinal Wyszyński (center) resisted the Nazis and did what he could to accommodate the Communists without sacrificing the church's authority. (AP Photo/ Girolamo di Majo)

later the aged cardinal gave support and encouragement to the reform-minded workers' union Solidarity. His influence helped to bring about the eventual collapse of communism in his country, an event he did not live to see.

everything they could to suppress the church. They threw priests and higher clerics into prison. They shut down churches, banned religious education, and restricted religious practices. But nothing could destroy the faith of the Polish people. The church had stood by them in times of crisis. Now they would stand by the church.

By 1956 the Communists realized they were fighting a losing battle. They ended the persecution and allowed religious worship to resume largely unhampered. The church was given more latitude than in any other communist country in Eastern Europe.

*A national religious icon, Our Lady of Częstochowa is also known as the Black Madonna because of the centuries of grime that have darkened the surface of this painting.*
(Courtesy Library of Congress)

## The Black Madonna of Częstochowa

To gain a better appreciation of the depth of the religious faith of Polish Catholics, one should visit Częstochowa, Poland's holiest city, in southwestern Poland. It is the home of the Black Madonna, a holy painting, supposedly done by Saint Luke and brought to a monastery on Jasna Góra, Mountain of Light, in the 14th century. The centuries have darkened the faces of the Virgin Mary and her child, the baby Jesus—hence, the name Black Madonna. According to legend, the monastery was attacked by Swedish soldiers during their invasion of Poland in 1655. Soldiers defended the monastery for 40 days until the invaders mysteriously retreated the day after Christmas. The Polish people attributed the miraculous retreat to the Black Madonna and rose up to beat back the Swedes from their land. Each year tens of thousands of Catholic Poles make the pilgrimage to the monastery during the yearly feast held in honor of Our Lady of Częstochowa.

## Polish Jews

Despite its long Catholic heritage, Poland has for centuries welcomed people of all faiths, making it one of the most tolerant countries in

Europe. Their own difficult history has made the Poles sensitive to all of society's victims and outcasts, especially those who have fled persecution for religious beliefs. Most prominent among these believers are the Jews.

Jews once made up 10 percent of the population of Poland, numbering 3.5 million. They included well-to-do peasants, artisans, and merchants, who could be found in every Polish city and town. The vast majority of Poland's Jews were killed in the Holocaust. Many others emigrated to escape extermination in the death camps. There are currently only 5,000 Jews left in Poland.

Despite their spirit of tolerance, Poles have also been guilty of anti-Semitism in the past, as have the people of nearly every European nation. Some Poles have even been accused of being indifferent to the plight of their Jewish neighbors during World War II. But there were many Poles who risked their own lives to help, too. Tadeusz Pankiewicz, a pharmacist in Kraków, is one outstanding example.

Pankiewicz was ordered by the Nazis in 1941 to leave Kraków's Jewish ghetto where his store was located. Somehow he persuaded the Germans to let him stay so he could continue selling medicine to the sick. Risking his life, he hid Jews in his pharmacy and stored sacred Torah and other Jewish artifacts in a vault under his store. When the war ended, Pankiewicz was a witness for the prosecution at the Nuremberg trials, where leading Nazis were prosecuted for war crimes.

Another hero of the Holocaust was Father Maximilian Kolbe, a Polish priest who took the place of a condemned man, a gentile, at Auschwitz. Kolbe was canonized as a saint by Pope John Paul.

But after more than half a century, the Holocaust continues to cause friction between Polish Catholics and Jews. Because so many Polish Catholics—1.5 million—died at Auschwitz, along with 2.5 million Jews, some Catholic Poles have resented the Jews claiming the Holocaust as exclusively "theirs." For one American Jewish scholar, the roots of the resentment run far deeper than that. "Poland sees itself as the Christ of nations," said Lucy S. Dawidowicz. "There is a sense among the Poles that the Jews are usurping Polish suffering."

This conflict came to a head in 1989, when Jewish Holocaust survivors urged the Catholic Church to remove a convent from the grounds of Auschwitz, claiming it was sacrilegious to their religion and suffering. The church vowed to remove the convent and then reneged on the promise. When a prominent Holocaust survivor denounced the church

## POPE JOHN PAUL II (b. 1920)

He is the world's most famous Pole, although he lives in Rome's Vatican City, hundreds of miles from his homeland. He is the first pope to come from a Communist country and probably will be the last. His intellect, fervent faith, and ceaseless energy have been an inspiration to millions of Catholics and non-Catholics the world over.

Pope John Paul II was born Karol Józef Wojtyla near Kraków in Wadowice. His father was an officer in the Polish army; his mother was Lithuanian. He was an outstanding scholar and athlete in school and popular with the girls. As a young man, he divided his time between working in a chemical factory and acting in amateur theatricals. His first passion was not the church but the theater.

For all his athletic vigor he nearly died twice before becoming a priest. He was knocked down by a streetcar, and a short time later was run over by a truck. The first accident left him with a fractured skull; the second, permanently stooped shoulders.

During the Nazi occupation, Wojtyla began studying for the priesthood in an underground seminary in Kraków and was ordained in 1946. A scholarly cleric with a keen intellect, he balanced the responsibilities of a parish priest with teaching duties at the Catholic University of Lublin and later the University of Kraków and, in 1964, was made archbishop of that city.

Fluent in five languages, including Latin, Karol Cardinal Wojtyla learned English in preparation for his first visit to the United States in 1969. In the 1970s he spoke out strongly against the Communist bureaucracy and was persecuted. In 1978 he became pope and a staunch defender of traditional church values. He traveled around the world to speak out against such issues as divorce, birth control, and women priests, although he also spoke out for freedom from communism, poverty, and political repression.

In 1981 this beloved pope was shot and wounded outside St. Peter's Church in the Vatican by a Turkish terrorist. He forgave his attacker, who later personally confessed his sin to him. His three visits to his native land in 1979, 1983, and 1988 inspired the Polish people and put continual pressure on the Communists to allow more freedom. Pope John Paul helped mediate the talks between the Communists and Solidarity that led to the fall of communism in Poland in 1989.

In the new, free Poland the pope remains a more inspiring leader than any politician, although his unyielding conservative stand on some issues is being questioned even by Polish Catholics.

In his best-selling book, *Crossing the Threshold of Hope* (1994), he describes himself as a "man of joy and a man of hope, a man of the fundamental affirmation of the value of existence, the value of creation and of hope in the future life."

At age 82, and in declining health, the pope made his ninth, and what some believe may be his last, papal trip to his native land in August 2002. Offering Mass before more than 2 million Poles in Kraków, an emotional John Paul said he would like to return but that "this is entirely in God's hands." The Polish people and much of the rest of the world continue to wish this remarkable man well.

*Author, playwright, scholar, and head of the Roman Catholic Church, Pope John Paul II is one of the most popular popes of the past century. He is also the most widely traveled pope in history.* (AP Photo/ Claudio Luffoli)

for its actions, conservative Polish Catholics urged the church not to give in to Jewish demands. This caused the primate, Józef Cardinal Glemp, the successor to Cardinal Wyszyński, to actually blame the "beloved Jews" for some of their own suffering. The convent was finally moved, but the incident has not been forgotten by either group.

More recently, during an audience with Pope John Paul II in June 1999, Polish rabbi Pinchas Menachem Joskowicz asked "Mr. Pope" to remove a large cross on one of the walls of Auschwitz. While many Jews felt the rabbi's timing was poor and his manner oafish, they agree that the Christian crosses at Auschwitz are an offense to their history and faith. While the Pope and other religious leaders continue to make efforts to bridge the gap separating Polish Catholics and Jews, problems remain.

## Other Religious Groups

Catholicism and Judaism are not the only religions represented in Poland today. There is a small minority of Protestants and members of the Eastern Orthodox Church. But the most interesting religious minority by far is the Polish National Catholic Church. This sect is made up of Poles who broke away from the Roman Catholic Church in the United States in 1897 in response to the church's poor record in Polish-American communities. Although Polish Catholics were contributing their energies and money to the church, there were, at the time, few Polish priests and no Polish bishops in the United States. The Polish National Catholic Church of America (PNCCA) remains the only major dissent group to break away from the Roman Catholic Church in the United States.

Missionaries from the new church first came to Poland in 1919. Twenty years later there were more than 50 parishes in Poland and a theological seminary in Kraków. In recent years the PNCCA has entered into talks with the Roman Catholic Church in Poland.

## The Church in Poland Today

Religion continues to be an important factor in the new Poland. However, the Catholic Church, once the defender of the people, has lost some of its luster now that communism has collapsed. As Western democratic ways have made inroads into Polish life, traditional values and the role of the church in Polish life are beginning to be questioned, as they are in other eastern European countries.

The church is no longer accepted as the single authority on social issues. The Democratic Union's support of the church's strict stand against abortion and for Catholic education in public schools was a contributing factor in its losing the election of 1992.

In 1995 the church backed Lech Wałesa in his reelection bid for president. Wałesa lost the presidency, and the church lost some of its luster. The election as president of Aleksander Kwaśniewski, a former Communist and avowed atheist, was a further blow to the church's authority.

"Kwaśniewski is not beholden to the Catholic Church," noted Polish journalist Konstanty Gebert. "Also, he desperately wants to strike the image of a modern, Western dynamic politician."

Cardinal Glemp has called Kwaśniewski and his party "neo-pagan," but enough Poles were impressed by his job performance to reelect him in 1999. Meanwhile, the church has had to face other challenges to its authority. The accusations of sexual abuse of young people by some Roman Catholic priests and higher clerics that swept across the United States in 2001 and 2002 have reverberated in Poland. In March 2002 Archbishop Juliusz Paetz of Poznań resigned after public accusations were made that he had molested young seminarians. Similar charges have been made against a number of Polish priests as well.

Whatever difficulties face the Catholic Church today, religion continues to be an important part of Polish life and will probably remain so as long as there is a Poland. As one 37-year-old pilgrim to Częstochowa said to a reporter, "Poland would not be Poland if it were not for the church."

## NOTES

p. 60 "'. . . the history of the Roman Catholic Church . . .'" Norman Davies. *God's Playground*, vol. 2 (New York: Columbia University Press, 1982), pp. 207–208.

p. 63 "'Poland sees itself . . .'" *Newsweek*, September 11, 1989, p. 36.

p. 65 "'man of joy . . .'" *New York Times*, October 20, 1994, p. A5.

p. 65 "'this is entirely in God's hands . . .'" *Connecticut Post*, August 19, 2002, p. D2.

p. 67 "'Kwaśniewski is not beholden . . .'" and "'neo-pagan.'" Jewish Bulletin of Northern California website. Available on-line. URL: http://jewishsf.com/bk951124/ipoles.htm. Downloaded August 26, 2003.

p. 67 "'Poland would not be Poland . . .'" *New York Times*, August 30, 1994, p. A5.

# 6

# THE ECONOMY

By 1998 the Polish economy was booming. It had become the envy of nearly every nation in postcommunist eastern Europe, including Russia. Of 11 American Enterprise Funds set up in eastern Europe by the United States to stimulate business, Poland was the only outstanding success. It was so successful that some Americans wanted the $240 million in investments made in Warsaw returned to the United States, feeling that the Poles did not need the money. With a 6 percent annual growth rate and unemployment low, Poland seemed well on the way to Western-style prosperity.

But by 2002 all that had changed. Hundreds of small businesses failed, unemployment hit 17 percent—an all-time high—and a deep pessimism eroded the public's faith in its government and its ability to make things better. Polish agriculture continued to be troubled by poor production and the threat of foreign imports. Government subsidies to farmers totaled $100 million a year.

What happened to throw the economy into such turmoil? There are a number of contributing factors. Part of the problem lies outside Poland. By 2000 a global economic slowdown affected many nations, including Russia, Germany, and the United States—three of Poland's leading export partners. As these countries bought fewer Polish goods, Poland's economy also faltered.

Meanwhile, as the hunger for Western consumer goods grew in Poland, so did the rush for credit to pay for these goods. Retail credit alone grew by 50 percent in 1997, although credit cards were still a rarity. Since then, however, credit card use has grown steadily from 7,000 cards in 2000 to 19,000 in 2001. But as the economy faltered, people could not pay off their debts.

In addition, "there is a deeper cultural problem of people wanting desperately to achieve Western living standards quickly, and no sense [that] this has consequences," said Marek Matraszek, director of the lobbying firm CEC in Warsaw. "You can't finance a Western life style with the gross domestic production per head of Poland."

Finally, thousands of small businesses flourished in the late 1990s but eventually overextended themselves, fell into debt, and then declared bankruptcy. "We almost choked on the belief that things would only get better," said Marek Kalinowski, owner of a chain of Warsaw clothing stores. "In my history as an entrepreneur, I only marched up, never down."

## The Economy under the Communists

Before looking closer at where the Polish economy is headed, it might do well to see where it has been. Before the Communists took control of the country, Poland was largely an agricultural society. Prior to the rebirth of the country after World War I, 60 percent of all Polish workers were farmers or agricultural laborers. Farms were small and far from productive. Poor soil and harsh winters made, and still make, farming a hard vocation. Many farming families subsisted on the potatoes, barley, and beets they grew and had little or nothing to sell as surplus. The Communists tried to force collectivization on the Polish farmers as they had in the Soviet Union. Large state-run farms were meant to replace small private ones. However, the stubborn, independent Polish farmers refused to give up the little they had. By the early 1950s the government gave up on trying to change them, and by 1986, in the last days of communism, 85 percent of all Polish farms were privately owned.

But the economy had changed. The Communists promoted industry to modernize the country and built up vast factories and industrial centers around such cities as Warsaw and Kraków. They stressed the production of capital goods—heavy machinery and factory equipment—over consumer goods—clothing, furniture, appliances, and cars

*Teenage boys herd cows from a pasture for milking near Kraków. Under the Communists most small farms like this one were privately owned.* (AP Photo/ Czarek Sokolowski)

for the people. Furthermore, much of what was manufactured in Poland was shipped out of the country to the Soviet Union. Polish goods did not benefit the Polish people, but the Russians. Novelist James Michener recalls this phenomenon in his travels in communist Poland:

> Wherever I had gone in those days it was the same. In Tarnow, boxcars carried farm produce into Russia. In Katowice, which I knew well from my visits, flatcars carried all the steel girders produced in the great Nowa Huta plants into Russia. In Gdansk, the fine new ships sailed to Russian home ports. Sometimes it seemed that nothing Polish produced remained at home.

However greedy the Soviets were, they did allow a certain amount of free enterprise in Poland. While the government ran 90 percent of all industry, the remaining 10 percent was owned by individuals and cooperative groups. This relatively high rate of private business, compared to the other Eastern bloc countries, was one important asset to the economy when communism fell in 1989.

# Small Businesses

Some small businesses began under communism and are now flourishing under capitalism. A small-business explosion continued from the 1990s into the beginning of the 21st century. "It seems that virtually anything that the elephantine state-run companies could not and would not provide under the Communists, Polish business people—and foreign friends—have provided since," wrote journalist Jane Perlez in 1998.

Marek Kamiński, an explorer and the first man to reach both the North and South Poles on foot in the same year (1995), is also co-owner of a growing bathroom equipment company. Another success story is the Grupa A5 company that designs other companies' labels and logos.

But for every successful new Polish business there are many that fail. Only 20 percent of young Polish entrepreneurs have the professional skills and know-how to succeed, according to Maciej Rydel, cofounder of Gdańsk Manager Training Foundation, one of Poland's first business schools. This and other business schools starting up in Poland are helping many young people gain the skills they need to compete. "An individual farmer or entrepreneur cannot count on the market," Rydel remarked at a business convention in Brussels, Belgium. "They must have representation that will fight for their place in Europe."

That fight does not appeal to many older Poles who remember the easier, if more repressive, time under the Soviet system when initiative was not encouraged or needed. In fact, one of Warsaw's most popular art exhibits in 2000 was a nostalgic reexamination of the Gomułka era entitled "Gray in Color: 1956–1970." It contained a socialist café that recalled the intellectual ferment as well as the spartan lifestyle of the period. Another significant exhibition was a Polish artist's parody of a U.S. supermarket that satirized rampant American consumerism. While Poland continues to work to achieve a free-market economy, ambiguous feelings about its simpler socialist past still linger.

# Agriculture

Agriculture, despite the many difficulties of raising crops, is also big business in Poland. It is the second largest producer of rye and potatoes in the world, after Russia. Barley, sugar beets, wheat, alfalfa, and clover are also important crops. Some grains are used to make Polish vodka, one of the most prized vodkas in the world. Livestock makes up two-fifths of total agricultural production. Hogs are raised throughout the country for processing as ham, sausage, and bacon. Sheep and cattle are raised for meat, wool, and milk in the grassy hills of the south.

## Natural Resources

While industry struggles to provide the consumer goods people want, Poland's natural resources are another area of vast untapped potential. Forests cover one-fourth of the country, but they have not been exploited to any great extent. Natural gas and petroleum deposits are more limited but have not been exploited, and 35 percent of Poland's fuel comes from other countries, most notably Russia.

One resource that has been used well is coal. Poland is the sixth largest coal-mining country and produced 114.5 million short tons (103.9

*President Aleksander Kwaśniewski hugs Polish Parliament speaker Marek Borowski on hearing the results of a national referendum in which a majority voted in favor of Poland's joining the European Union (EU). First Lady Jolanta Kwaśniewska looks just as pleased with the outcome.* (AP Photo/ Czarek Sokolowski)

million metric tons) of coal in 2001. The coalfield around the city of Katowice is one of the largest in the world. However, in 2000 the government closed 22 coal mines and partially closed seven others in an effort to restructure the industry and make it more efficient. Poland also has smaller amounts of copper, lead, zinc, sulfur, and salt.

## The European Union

The European Union (EU), a trade bloc of 15 European nations, is presently Poland's best hope for a brighter economic future. At a summit meeting held in Copenhagen, Denmark, at the end of 2002, the EU made its final decision to allow Poland and nine other nations, mostly in eastern Europe, to join the EU in May 2004.

The largest of the applying countries, Poland demanded and received huge concessions from the EU. They include $1.53 billion in financial assistance between 2004 and 2006, much of it going to subsidize Polish farmers who fear their livelihood will be jeopardized by imported agricultural products once Poland joins the union.

In a national referendum on Poland's entry to the EU, held in June 2003, an overwhelming majority of 82 percent of votes cast were in favor of joining. "We are coming back," declared a jubilant President Kwaśniewski. "We are coming back to Europe." Kwaśniewski now has the popular mandate he needed to ratify the treaty with the EU and complete the membership process.

**NOTES**

p. 70 "'There is a deeper cultural problem . . .'" *New York Times*, May 30, 1998, p. A3.

p. 70 "'We almost choked on the belief . . .'" *New York Times*, August 16, 2002, p. A6.

p. 71 "'Wherever I had gone . . .'" James Michener. *Pilgrimage: A Memoir of Poland and Rome* (Emmaus, Pa.: Rodale Press, 1990), pp. 20–21.

p. 72 "'It seems that virtually anything . . .'" *New York Times*, September 23, 1998, p. 5.

p. 72 "'An individual farmer or entrepreneur . . .'" Warsaw Voice-Business website. Available on-line. URL: http://www.warsawvoice.pl/old/v477/Busiol.html. Downloaded August 29, 2003.

p. 74 "'We are coming back, . . .'" Halifax Herald Limited. Available on-line. URL: http://www.herald.ns.ca/stories/2003/06/09/fWorld115.raw.html. Downloaded August 25, 2003.

*7*

# Culture

⤜⤛

The coming of Christianity to Poland in A.D. 966 did much more than make Poland a Catholic country. It also made it, despite its location in the heart of eastern Europe, very much a Western nation. Along with priests and missionaries, the pope in Rome sent artists and scholars from the center of western Europe to Poland. These people spread Western views and styles that had a profound effect on Polish architecture, literature, art, music, science, law, and education.

Because of their vulnerability to enemies, Poles have cultivated a strong sense of patriotism and national pride over the centuries. Polish culture, particularly its literature and art, have followed suit. The most characteristic works of Poland's finest artists and writers until recently reflected national concerns and themes more than personal and individual ones. Poland's creative minds have traditionally tended to look more outward than inward.

## Language

Among European languages, Polish is one of the most formidable looking to nonspeakers with its strange combinations of consonants and vowels. A Slavic language, similar to Russian, Polish has 10 vowels and 35 consonants. It has been enriched over the centuries with vocabulary from German, Italian, French, English, and Ukrainian. Polish is spoken by more than 38 million people in the world today, including about 3 million in the United States.

# Literature

The first great flowering of Polish literature and the other arts was in the 16th century under the Jagiellonian kings during the nation's golden age. It perhaps reached its pinnacle in the poetry of Jan Kochanowski (1530–84). This versatile writer adapted the poetic traditions of France and Italy and fashioned from them a poetic language that raised Polish literature to new heights. His poems cover an extraordinary range of subjects and moods, from stirring patriotic lyrics to sorrowful elegies to his dead daughter. Kochanowski even wrote a Polish version of the Bible's Book of Psalms.

The second golden age of Polish literature came not when Poland was at the height of greatness but at its nadir. During the 19th century, when Poland had ceased to exist as a nation, poets and novelists kept the flame of Polish nationalism alive in epic novels and poems about the greatness of their country's past. Poet Adam Mickiewicz (1798–1855) symbolized Poland's fight with Russia in his epic poem *Konrad Wallenrod* about the earlier wars with the Teutonic Knights. An exile for much of his adult life, Mickiewicz was arrested and exiled by the Russians for "spreading wrong-headed Polish nationalism" through his early poems and political activities. Henry Sienkiewicz (1846–1916), who became the first Polish writer to win the Nobel Prize in literature in 1905, wrote a trilogy about Poland's struggle against invaders in the 17th century.

Another great Polish writer was Władysław Stanisław Reymont (1867–1926), who wrote movingly of Poland's poor and underprivileged. Born into grinding poverty in a peasant village, Reymont escaped into a make-believe world of theater when he joined a troupe of traveling actors. This experience served as the basis for his first novel, *The Comedienne* (1896). His masterpiece is his four-volume epic *The Peasants* (1902–09) that shows the heroic character of Poland's simple villagers. For this and other works, Reymont became the second Pole, after Sienkiewicz, to win the Nobel Prize in literature, in 1924.

With the rebirth of Poland in 1919, a group of urban poets who called themselves the Skamander group encouraged Polish writers to look inward and abandon traditional forms for more experimental ones. This new movement was short-lived, however. The German occupation during World War II dealt a terrible blow to Polish culture and the arts. The nightmarish war years were poignantly captured in the terse concentration camp stories of Tadeusz Borowski (1922–51). At age 21, Borowski was imprisoned in Auschwitz and Dachau for two years. In *This Way for the Gas, Ladies and Gentlemen*, Borowski describes the arrival of a trainload of doomed Jews at his camp:

> The bolts crack, the doors fall open. A wave of fresh air rushes inside the train. People . . . inhumanly crammed, buried under incredible heaps of luggage, suitcases, trunks, packages, crates, bundles of every description (everything that had been their past and was to start their future). Monstrously squeezed together, they have fainted from heat, suffocated, crushed one another. Now they push towards the opened doors, breathing like fish cast out on the sand. . . .
>
> A huge, multicolored wave of people loaded down with luggage, pours from the train like a blind, mad river trying to find a new bed. But before they have a chance to recover, before they can draw a breath of fresh air and look at the sky, bundles are snatched from their hands, coats ripped off their backs, their purses and umbrella taken away. . . .
>
> The heaps grow. Suitcases, bundles, blankets, coats, handbags that open as they fall, spilling coins, gold, watches; mountains of bread pile up at the exits, heaps of marmalade, jams, masses of meat, sausages; sugar spills on the gravel. Trucks, loaded with people, start up with a deafening roar and drive off amidst the wailing and screaming of the women separated from their children, and the stupefied silence of the men left behind. They are the ones who had been ordered to step to the right—the healthy and the young who will go to the camp. In the end, they too will not escape death, but first they must work.
>
> Trucks leave and return, without interruption, as on a monstrous conveyor belt. A Red Cross van drives back and forth, back and forth, incessantly: it transports the gas that will kill these people. The enormous cross on the hood, red as blood, seems to dissolve in the sun.

*Poet Wisława Szymborska joyfully accepts the Polish PEN literary club's annual prize in Warsaw on September 30, 1996. Three days later she received an even greater honor: the Nobel Prize in literature. (AP Photo/Filip Miller)*

Borowski survived the death camps, but they haunted him the rest of his life. Disillusioned with the new communist regime that turned him into a propagandist hack, Borowski committed suicide by gas asphyxiation three day after his wife, who had survived the camps with him, gave birth to their daughter.

Five years later a thaw in the communist regime allowed a certain amount of creative freedom to writers and intellectuals, although that freedom had its limits. Some of the best contemporary writers during the communist era chose to turn away from realism toward fantasy and satire in order to criticize the communist system indirectly. In his satirical plays and fablelike stories, Sławomir Mrozek (b. 1936) savaged the Communists and their bureaucracy in a comic and entertaining style. Another writer, Stanisław Lem (b. 1921), turned to surrealistic science fiction to escape the grimness of communist Poland. Czesław Miłosz (b. 1911) is Poland's most celebrated contemporary poet, but he is best known in the West for his essay "The Captive Mind," a stinging critique of communism. Miłosz won the Nobel Prize in literature in 1980.

Fellow Polish poet Wisława Szymborska (b. 1923), the author of 16 volumes of verse, won the Nobel Prize in literature in 1996. In her Nobel lecture Szymborska had this to say about the nature of her craft:

Poets if they're genuine, must also keep repeating "I don't know." Each poem marks an effort to answer this statement, but as soon as the final period hits the page, the poet begins to hesitate, starts to realize that this particular answer was pure makeshift that's absolutely inadequate to boot. So the poets keep on trying. . . .

And so Poland's contemporary writers, with insight and courage, continue to try to make sense out of an increasingly senseless world.

# Music

While literature was an inspiration for 19th-century Poles, it was the stirring polonaises and mazurkas of Frédéric Chopin (see boxed biography) that best expressed Polish patriotism for the rest of the Western world. While Chopin's exquisite piano works reflect his deep love of his homeland, many of his other compositions, particularly his études, reflect deeply personal feelings that looked forward to the modernism of the 20th century.

Polish classical music in the 20th century more directly mirrored the violence and political upheavals that the country experienced. Perhaps Poland's best-known modern composer, Krzysztof Penderecki (b. 1933), wrote the stirring *Threnody for the Victims of Hiroshima* (1960), a tribute from a Polish war survivor to other victims of that war half a world away.

## FRÉDÉRIC CHOPIN (1810–1849)

He was not a great performer, he never mastered the classical form of the symphony, and he died of tuberculosis before he was 40. But no classical composer of the 19th century was a greater master of piano composition than Frédéric Chopin.

Chopin was born in Zelazona-Wola, near Warsaw, to a French father and a Polish mother. He was a child prodigy and wrote his first composition, a polonaise—a kind of stately Polish dance—at age seven. He gave his first public concert the following year. After graduating from the Warsaw Conservatory, Chopin traveled abroad and settled in Paris in 1831. Too sickly to perform much, he earned a living teaching wealthy women the piano while composing. Although he wrote sonatas, waltzes, and two piano concertos, Chopin's best-known and most-loved compositions are his 40 mazurkas, Polish folk dances, and 15 polonaises. These pieces burst with national pride and a deep love for his native land, which he never saw again after the age of 20.

In 1837 Chopin met and fell in love with Aurore Dupin, the novelist better known to the world by her pseudonym, George Sand. They were an unlikely match—the strong, masculine Sand who liked to scandalize society by smoking cigars in public and the weak, refined Chopin. However, their relationship lasted nine years, and Sand was

A restless innovator, Penderecki has incorporated typewriting, sawing wood, and hissing singers into his works.

Witold Lutosławski (1913–94) used elements of Polish folk music in his work and won a Grammy in the United States in 1986 for a recording of his *Symphony No. 3*. Henryk Górecki (b. 1933), another popular composer, wrote his *Miserere* to commemorate the police violence against Solidarity in 1981 and paid musical tribute to the pope's third visit to his homeland in 1987 in his *Totus Tuus*.

Among contemporary Polish composers, few are as gifted and prolific as Wojciech Kilar (b. 1932). Known for such outstanding classical works as his *Piano Concerto* (1997), Kilar has also composed more than 100 film scores, including those for such recent motion pictures as Andrzej Wajda's *Zemsta* (*The Revenge*) (2002) and Roman Polanski's Oscar-winning *The Pianist* (2002).

the great love of Chopin's life. Her tender care and attention helped him conserve his energies for composing many of his finest works. When they separated in 1846, Chopin's health declined, and he all but gave up composing.

Chopin left France for England two years later and briefly revived his career on the concert stage. He even gave a private perform-ance for Queen Victoria. One of his last concerts was fittingly a benefit for Polish refugees. He died in Paris of tuberculosis, the disease that had haunted him for years, on October 17, 1849. A year later a monument of a weeping Muse with a broken lyre was erected over his grave. When it was dedicated, a tiny box of Polish soil was sprinkled on the grave. The exile had come home at last.

*The sensitive nature of composer Frédéric Chopin is captured in this portrait.* (Courtesy Library of Congress)

# Art

Polish visual artists have not often shared in the international fame of their compatriot writers and composers. The first Polish painter to have a worldwide reputation was Jan Matejko (1838–93). What Mickiewicz and Sienkiewicz achieved in literature, Matejko realized in his huge his-torical paintings, which depict some of the finest moments in Polish history. One French critic described Matejko's work as

enormous canvases, fifteen or twenty feet long, encumbered with people in diverse costumes, full of bizarre details, spotted with brilliant colors, which are piled one on the other so that the air and the light cannot play between them. At first the eye suffers from this tumult, then one discovers an original composition, great firmness of drawing, energetic and free attitudes, and figures of surprising rudeness.

Polish artists in the 20th century turned away from the grandeur of epic painting to the more contained but equally propagandistic art of the poster. Chief among these poster artists is Franciszek Starowieyski whose weird fantastic art includes the repeated imagery of disembodied eyeballs, spiders, and skulls. Starowieyski's work, according to one art review in the *New York Times*, "catches a sense of nonrelieved gloom that might easily be seen to reflect a repressive society that wasn't working very well."

The most exciting development in the Polish art world since the fall of communism is the opening in 1990 of the Center for Contemporary Art, located in 17th-century Ujazdowski Castle. "This museum is a kind of laboratory of the arts; it is a space for art in progress," said its director and Solidarity supporter Wojciech Krukowski. Shows such as a comparison of Stalinist social realism paintings with huge Polish installation art of the 1980s, and a comprehensive look at Polish art of the 1990s, have given the museum an international reputation.

One of the more intriguing contemporary Polish artists is Grozyna Lippert-Zajaczkowska (b. 1954) who is known for her mixed media work that blends the traditional with the modern. Typical is her *The Year 2000* (2000), a triptych that juxtaposes the image of a medieval church with, among others, an aerial photo of Chicago's Navy Pier. "In some of my paintings," she explains, "I adopted the structure of a medieval altar merging external shape of the painting with its internal motif, and its encrusted surface pattern figures."

# Film and Theater

Polish filmmakers have also had a strong interest in the macabre and the gruesome, perhaps none more so than French-born Polish director Roman Polanski (b. 1933). Polanski, who was born Jewish, had a horrible childhood in war-torn Poland. His parents were taken to a concentration camp when he was eight, and he wandered the countryside finding shelter from the storm with a series of Catholic families. After the war Polanski studied film at the famous Polish Film School at Łódź, where most of Poland's best directors got their start. After making several surreal shorts and a superb psychological thriller, *Knife in the Water* (1962), Polanski left Poland and eventually came to Hollywood, where he made such classic horror and crime films as *Rosemary's Baby* (1968) and *Chinatown* (1974). In 1981 Polanski returned to Poland and directed and starred in Peter Shaffer's play *Amadeus* in Warsaw. His most recent film, *The Pianist* (2002), based on the life of Polish Jewish musician Władysław Szpilman, who survived World War II in the Warsaw Ghetto, won Polanski an Academy Award for best director. Its star, Adrian Brody, received the Oscar for best actor.

While veteran directors like Andrzej Wajda (see boxed biography) and Krzysztof Kieslowski (1941–96) continued to probe Poland's past and present in personal and political dramas and war films, younger directors such as Władysław Pasikowski have moved in other directions. His action thriller *Dogs 2* (1993), about a Pole's involvement with the Russian Mafia, is one of the biggest box-office hits in postcommunist Poland. "When someone says my movies are Hollywoodish, I consider that a great compliment," says Pasikowski. "My role is not to preach, just to tell a story."

*Film director Andrzej Wajda (left) shares a press conference with fellow filmmaker Roman Polanski, who appeared in Wajda's 2002 film* Zemsta (The Revenge). *Polanski began his film career 47 years earlier, acting in Wajda's first full-length feature film,* Pokolenie (A Generation). (AP Photo/Alik Keplicz)

Polish cinema reached a landmark with the 1999 release of *With Fire and Sword*, a national epic based on the famous historical novel by Henryk Sienkiewicz. An $8.5 million production, it is the most expensive film ever made in Poland.

In Polish theater one of the most influential and innovative artists is Jerzy Grotowski (1934–99), founder and director of the Wrocław Labo-

---

### ANDRZEJ WAJDA (b. 1926)

Few 20th-century artists have plumbed the depths of the Polish national character as deeply and passionately as filmmaker Andrzej Wajda. Poland's most distinguished director for four decades, his motion pictures wrestle with the forces that have both inspired and ravaged his nation.

Wajda's father was a cavalry officer who died on the battlefield in World War II. At 16, Wajda became a Resistance fighter against the Nazis, who occupied his country. When Poland was liberated after the war, he was an art student at the Kraków Academy of Fine Arts and later enrolled in the famous Łódź film school. After graduating in 1952, he worked as an assistant to Polish filmmaker Aleksander Ford, director of Film Polski, the government-run film organization.

Wajda's first full-length film, *A Generation* (1954), dealt with Polish youth resistance during the Nazi occupation and was largely based on his own experiences. It proved to be the first part of a memorable war trilogy. *Kanal* (1957) told in gripping detail the story of a group of Resistance fighters during the Warsaw Uprising, trying to escape through the city's underground sewers. *Ashes and Diamonds* (1958) was even more searing, as a doomed Polish nationalist struggles with his last assignment—the assassination of a leading bureaucrat who has sold out to the Communists in postwar Poland. Wajda boldly set the final death scene of the assassin, played by Zbigniew Cybulski, the Polish James Dean, against lines of white laundry and heaps of rubble.

Wajda's subsequent movies have ranged from pointed comedies to historical films and contemporary political dramas. His best films have looked unflinchingly at the futility of war and the waste of heroism. For all his bitter cynicism, Wajda has never given up hope for the future of his country. When the first freely elected Polish parliament took office in 1989, among its most celebrated members was the filmmaker Wajda.

ratory Theater. Grotowski's "poor theater" reduced play performance to the absolute essentials, doing away with costumes, makeup, lighting, and sound effects.

## Folk Art and Music

There is a side to Polish culture that does not stem from individual artists and writers but from the common people. While the cities have largely lost touch with the folk art and music of Poland, both still flourish in the villages and small towns of the countryside. The Kurpianka Cepelia Cooperative was established in 1950 to encourage folk artists to make and sell their tapestries, wood carvings, pottery, and other folk art pieces at specialty shops called Cepelia stores. The cooperative also supports village musicians in the Green Forest song and dance ensemble. Other folk festivals keep this very lively but complicated music alive from the Tatra region to Kaimierz, a town on the banks of the Vistula River.

As Poland enters a new era of freedom, old problems and issues will give way to new ones. These will be examined and reflected in Polish culture, a culture that has been a comfort and a support to its people in both good times and bad.

### NOTES

p. 79 "'The bolts crack . . .'" Tadeusz Borowski. *This Way for the Gas, Ladies and Gentlemen* (New York: Penguin, 1976), pp. 37–38.

p. 81 "'Poets if they're genuine . . .'" Nobel e-Museum. Available on-line. URL: http://www.nobel.se/literature/laureates/1996/szymborska-lecture.html. Downloaded August 25, 2003.

p. 84 "'enormous canvases . . .'" *Artists of the 19th Century and Their Works* (Boston: Houghton Mifflin, 1899), p. 99.

p. 84 "'catches a sense of nonrelieved gloom . . .'" *New York Times*, May 16, 1993, n.p.

p. 84 "'This museum is a kind of laboratory . . .'" *New York Times*, September 19, 1997, n.p.

p. 84 "'In some of my paintings . . .'" ArtScope.net. Available on-line. URL: http://www.artscope.net/VAREVIEWS/athenaeumo700_l.shtml. Downloaded August 26, 2003.

p. 86 "'When someone says my movies . . .'" *New York Times*, April 30, 1994, p. 13.

# 8

# DAILY LIFE

Daily life in Poland is not easy. Under communism Poles were deprived of the most basic consumer goods and comforts. Now, caught between a planned economy that never worked and a free-market one that is still evolving, Poland's standard of living remains low compared to the United States and most countries in western Europe. The fervent complaint of Halina Bortnowska, a lay Catholic activist from Kraków, echoes the feelings of millions of ordinary Poles:

> We live from one day to the next, and we've been doing it for too long—for years now—and we're tired, we're exhausted. Every morning, I wake up and wonder, Is my washing machine going to work today? . . . on that day [that it doesn't] my standard of living will take a decisive plunge. Because I'll never be able to afford a new one, not ever again. . . . And every day, waking up, I wonder, Is this going to be the day? *About everything.* And this is no way to live.

Another woman, Joanna Jedraszkiewicz, who lost her job as a graphic designer, was even more pessimistic. "I am 50 and have no future. What are they going to do with my generation? Shoot them?"

Despite these problems, most Poles, as they have so many times in the past, keep their faith and try to look forward to a better future. In the meantime, they continue to work hard, play hard, and wait.

# Housing

Adequate housing continues to be a major problem for many Poles, especially in the cities, where the majority of people live in apartments. Many urban apartment buildings are old, overcrowded, and in desperate need of repair: About 41 percent of all apartments were built before 1960. According to a 2000 survey taken by the Public Opinion Research Center, 35 percent of respondents said their building needed major repairs. Some 14 percent of the respondents live in apartments with more than two people per room. Young married couples are particularly affected by the housing shortage. Many of them are forced to live with their parents or grandparents.

The government attempted to improve the situation with the Housing Act of 1995, which provides housing allowances for those people who cannot afford a home. However, many Poles do not know about the allowances due to poor communication, and only 6 percent of the people have so far received them. Other Poles are too proud to seek financial assistance, although a majority of the population thinks the government should help solve the housing problem. Other solutions include an increase in housing construction and a lowering of housing costs.

# Education

Education is important in Poland and always has been. With the collapse of communism, Marxist indoctrination ended in schools and a free exchange of ideas began. Elementary school—from ages seven to 15—is compulsory in Poland. Secondary school, roughly the equivalent of American high school, begins at age 16 and runs four years. In secondary school, the workload increases, and students are expected to choose a special field of study, much as American students do in college. Both elementary and secondary students must attend a half day of school on Saturdays. Education is free up to the university level.

There are a number of other differences in the way schools are run in Poland as compared to those in the United States. When students enter their classroom, for instance, they remove their shoes in the cloakroom and put on special slippers they will wear all day at school. These help to keep the school's floors clean. Although most elementary students take six subjects, including a foreign language, they remain in one classroom all day. The teachers are the ones who go from room to room each period.

Teachers are strict and class procedure is more formal than in most U.S. schools. If a student misbehaves or breaks a rule, it is announced publicly to the entire student body. The shame and embarrassment the student experiences will, it is hoped, prevent him or her from repeating such behavior.

Those students who do well academically in secondary school and pass the stringent entrance exams, go on to study at one of Poland's 102 institutions of higher learning, including universities and many specialized and technical schools. The university system has been plagued by many problems. Teachers and administrators are poorly paid, and some of them are incompetent. In 1990 only $1,200 were spent on educating one student per year in Poland, compared to $12,000 spent per student per year in the United States. Many Polish youth have been unable to gain admission to a university because there are so few places and the competition is fierce. In June 2001 the Sejm passed the Act of Higher Education, which called for an increase of salaries over three years and created the State Accreditation Commission to establish new institutions and assess teaching quality and set new standards. Nonetheless, despite problems the Polish government and people have made education a priority. In the 2001–02 academic year there were 1,718,700 students enrolled in institutions of higher learning.

## Women's Issues

The transition from communism to an open, democratic society has not been kind to Polish women. While feminism by Western standards was not a part of the Soviet system, women had nominal equality with men, were allowed to receive an education, and played prominent roles in the workplace and in politics. Before independence women made up 30 percent of the members of the Sejm; by 2000 that figure had dropped to 13.7 percent, or 63 women out of 460 members. Under communism

Poland had a Ministry of Women in the government; in postcommunist Poland it has been replaced by a Ministry for the Family. Child care for working women, once universal, is now limited. The right to abortion, granted under communism, ended in 1993 when a strict ban on abortions was passed. It was amended in 1997, allowing abortions when the mother's life was endangered or when the pregnancy resulted from rape or incest. At present many Polish women seeking abortions travel across the border to the Czech Republic where abortion is legal.

Perhaps the most disturbing trend in women's issues is the apparent rise in domestic violence. Spousal abuse has long been a problem in this patriarchal society, but lately it has been getting worse as unemployed husbands take out their frustrations on their families. The number of reported cases of abuse rose 33 percent in 1995. This may be partly due to a new openness in Polish society, with more women reporting abuse for the first time. In 2000, Polish police reported 23,147 cases of family abuse with 161 cases of extremely severe abuse.

A Women's Rights Center has been established in Warsaw, but in 1998 there were no battered women's centers in the city. Many women remain trapped in abusive marriages because divorce is still difficult in this staunchly Catholic nation. The critical housing shortage and women's economic dependence on their husbands make leaving home often impossible. Some of those women who have been bold enough to assert themselves have been abandoned by their husbands and left alone with children in dire economic and psychological straits.

But a growing awareness of women's rights is beginning to make a difference. "Slowly there has started to be a feminist movement here," noted leading Polish stage and screen actress Krystyna Janda. Successful, activist women like Janda and Polish first lady Jolanta Kwaśniewska have given Polish women something they have rarely had in the past—role models.

## Sports and Recreation

Soccer is Poland's most popular sport, and it is played in every school. Professional soccer is Poland's most popular spectator sport, and crowds flock to the giant sports stadium in Warsaw and in other cities to see teams in Poland's two pro divisions play. Volleyball and basketball are other popular team sports, while gymnastics, swimming, and ice skating are the favorite individual sports. Table tennis and tennis have also become popular with young people in recent years.

Polish athletes have traditionally done well at the Olympic Games. At the 2000 Summer Games, in Sydney, Australia, Poland won a total of 14 medals, including six gold medals. At the 2002 Winter Games at Salt Lake City, Utah, Polish ski jumper Adam Małysz won a silver medal and a bronze medal in two events.

Most Poles enjoy the outdoors. During summer vacation, many city families travel south to the Tatra Mountains, a popular vacation area. They spend their time enjoying nature, which they don't get to see much of the rest of the year. They go on hikes, canoe, and swim. To get out of the city, many young people hitchhike. Poland is one of the few Western countries where hitchhiking is not only legal but also encouraged by the government. A hitchhiking committee issues coupon books to hitchhikers. When a driver picks him or her up, the hitchhiker gives the person coupons from the book. At the end of the year those drivers with the highest number of coupons are awarded prizes.

## Food and Drink

Eating is a serious business in Poland. Polish cuisine is one of the best-kept secrets in Europe. Each conquering group dominating Poland brought dishes from home, which the Poles adapted to their own cuisine. This blending has made Polish cooking one of the most interesting and original in the world. Americans, even those of Polish descent, who think Polish food begins and ends with the sausage kielbasa and stuffed dumplings called pierogis may be surprised to learn the great range and variety of Polish food.

Polish families gather around the dining table for their biggest meal of the day, *obiad*, or dinner. Many families share this meal most nights around 5:00 P.M., but some eat as early as 3:00 or 4:00 P.M., depending on their work schedules.

Polish dinners often begin with a bowl of soup. Poles love homemade soup and make an astounding variety of it. A national favorite is *barszcz*, or beet soup. It consists of pork and beef stock, diced pickled beets, and dried mushrooms, with a generous dollop of sour cream, a favorite garnish, on top. In the hot summer months Poles relish cold soups made from native fruits.

Soup is followed by the main dish: beef, ham, or perhaps baked fish. Fish may seem an odd entrée in a largely landlocked country, but Poland's many lakes abound with carp, pike, and cod, while herring comes from the chilly Baltic Sea. The fish is cooked in a mushroom sauce. Mushrooms grow wild in many parts of Poland, and picking them is a favorite family activity. Along with the main course are boiled potatoes and perhaps stuffed tomatoes. Dinner ends with a rich dessert such as *naleszniki*, thin pancakes stuffed with fruit.

Tea is the favorite beverage of Poles, while vodka is the most popular alcoholic drink. Poland is the third largest market for vodka after Russia and the United States. In 1998 vodka consumption was nearly seven quarts (6.86 liters) per capita.

## The Media

Poland's more than 80 newspapers have flourished in the wake of communism. Once mere mouthpieces of the government and forced to follow the party line, journalists have taken to honest, investigative work with a vengeance. They have exposed the corruption and other crimes of the new Polish politicians and alerted the public to threatened encroachments on personal freedoms from former Communists in power.

Polish television has come a long way since the dreary days of communism. There are still two state channels, but the introduction of cable TV has brought a far greater variety of programming on the more than 13 million television sets in the country. With 1.2 million cable customers, Poland is the seventh largest cable user in Europe today. Polish youth enjoy MTV, while their parents favor such shows as *Kolo Fortuna*, the Polish version of the U.S. game show *Wheel of Fortune*.

In 1998 there were 14 AM and 777 FM radio stations broadcasting to more than 20 million radios. Some 6.4 million Poles used the Internet in 2001, and there were 19 Internet service providers in 2000.

# Holidays

While daily life can be a grind for many Poles, there are a number of holidays throughout the year that offer them a chance to relax and celebrate.

The two biggest holidays in Poland are Christmas and Easter. Christmas is more than a holiday to the Poles; it is an entire season that begins on St. Martin's Day, November 12, and continues until Twelfth Night on January 6. The nearly two months between these two dates are filled with religious services, feasting, celebrating, and gift giving.

*Children wearing colorful holiday costumes play and sing Christmas carols from house to house in the snowy Polish countryside.* (Courtesy Polish National Tourist Office)

Roast goose is the traditional fare on St. Martin's Day, while St. Andrew's Day (November 30) resembles an autumnal St. Valentine's Day. Young men and women wear cherry blossoms on this day and bestow them on their sweethearts. According to another folk tradition, young people put a twig from a cherry tree into a cup of water. If the twig blooms before the new year, they will find romance and happiness in the coming year.

St. Nicholas Day, December 6, is the traditional day of gift giving, as it is in many European countries. Children receive religious pictures, presents, and pastries. As Christmas draws nearer, the households become filled with the smell of *pierniki*, honey cakes baked in the shape of animals and Nativity scenes. They are baked and stored away to be aged and eaten on Christmas Eve. While Christmas carolers traditionally entertain families in other countries during the Christmas season, in Poland puppeteers go from house to house acting out the Nativity story for children and their parents in exchange for cookies and a cup of good cheer.

*An elderly woman decorates Easter eggs, or* pisanki, *for the most important religious holiday in Poland.* (Courtesy Free Library of Philadelphia)

On Christmas Eve the entire season reaches its culmination. Many Catholics fast all day in anticipation of the evening feast. Christmas Eve dinner, the *wigilia*, is traditionally meatless and includes baked fish, beet soup, potato dumplings, cabbage, and numerous rich desserts. Hearty appetites may have no qualms about overindulging, for it is bad luck not to taste every dish. After eating, the family sings Christmas carols and opens gifts. The memorable night ends with everyone attending midnight mass at the local church.

Christmas Day, as it is in many places, is a more quiet time spent with family and friends. Food is cooked in advance so no one has to work in the kitchen. A Christmas favorite is *bigos*, or hunter's stew, a savory blend of sausage, sauerkraut, pork, cabbage, and spices, that can take up to a week to cook.

New Year's Eve, known as Sylvester in Poland, is marked by parties and balls filled with music and dancing. Special almond cakes have coins baked inside them. Those who find a coin will have good luck in the new year.

Easter is a time of prayer and *pisanki*, Polish Easter eggs. These decorated eggs are something of a fine art with their rich designs and bold colors. They are used, along with flowers, to decorate the Easter table, which groans with ham, sausage, vegetables, soups, and wines. On Holy Saturday, the day before Easter Sunday, parishioners take decorated baskets of food to the local church to be blessed by the priest. A special Easter dish is butter made into the shape of a lamb, the symbol of Christ, with cloves for eyes, lying on a green bed of parsley.

Easter Monday, in sharp contrast to the previous day's solemnity, is a time of high spirits and romance—both signs of the coming of spring. Boys and men spray water or perfume on their sweethearts or wives. It is a good example of how pagan rites mingle with Christian ones on Polish holidays.

Life in Poland is full bodied and hearty, like a rich Polish soup. Here, the ordinary and the extraordinary, the sacred and the profane exist in the same simmering bowl.

## NOTES

p. 89 "'We live from one day to the next . . .'" Lawrence Weschler, "Deficit," *New Yorker*, May 11, 1992, p. 60.

p. 89 "'I am 50 . . .'" *New York Times*, September 18, 1993, p. 4.

p. 92 "'Slowly there has started . . .'" *New York Times*, February 16, 1995, p. B1.

# 9

# CITIES

A nation's achievements and aspirations are often best reflected in its cities. The devastation and destruction that Poland experienced in World War II, under German occupation, nearly obliterated its cities and all they represented. City after city was burned, plundered, and razed by the Nazis.

## Warsaw—The City That Wouldn't Die

No Polish metropolis suffered more in World War II than its largest city and capital, Warsaw. Ninety percent of the city's buildings were destroyed. Two-thirds of its population were killed or imprisoned. Centuries-old buildings were reduced to rubble and ash. By war's end Warsaw was a burned shell of its former self.

The people of Warsaw might have been expected to start over and build modern high-rise apartments and office buildings on the sites of ancient churches and palaces. But anyone who thought that did not know the Poles' love of their great city. Using old photographs, pictures, and architectural designs and plans, they lovingly re-created an exact replica of Warsaw as it had been before the war. Today Warsaw is a modern city that retains much of its old-world charm and dignity, thanks to the painstaking efforts of its residents.

Warsaw (population 1,607,600)* is situated in central Poland and is divided in two by the Vistula River. The river, according to legend, played a major role in the city's founding. A fisherman, so the story goes, was fishing on the banks of the Vistula when a mermaid appeared to him. The sea creature told him that one day a great city would be built on the very spot where he stood. The fisherman, named Warsz, gave his name to the city, and the mermaid is still commemorated in the city's coat of arms.

The first record of the historical Warsaw appeared in the 900s when a small settlement inhabited by Slavic tribes was noted. A few hundred years later Warsaw became the official residence of the dukes of Mazovia, a family of Polish nobles. In 1596 King Sigismund III moved his capital from Kraków to Warsaw when Mazovia became part of his kingdom.

As Poland's fortunes fell in the 17th century, so did Warsaw's. Swedish invaders destroyed much of the city in 1656. It ceased to be a capital when the Prussians took it over in the final partition of Poland in 1795. The city briefly emerged to become the capital of Napoléon's Duchy of Warsaw in 1807. Russia regained control of the territory six years later and relegated Warsaw to obscurity once again.

The city was, nevertheless, a hotbed of national resistance in the 19th century and was the scene of two aborted rebellions in 1830 and 1863. Control of Warsaw passed from Russia to Germany in World War I, ending in its independence in 1918. The Nazis laid siege to the city in 1939 and devastated it. Warsaw's residents surrendered but never admitted defeat. Warsaw became the hub of the Polish Underground resistance.

In the war's final days, knowing they faced imminent defeat, the Nazis exacted their final revenge on the city. They burned and blew up those buildings that had eluded destruction in five years of conflict. The Soviets, who could have saved Warsaw from this last indignity, waited outside the city and moved in to "liberate" it only on January 17, 1945, when the Germans had finished. Memories of the war years can still be seen everywhere. Statues, monuments, and memorials to the war dead dot the city. Most moving of all are the flower-laden plaques, marking the spots where Poles were killed during the war.

---

*All populations given in this chapter are 2003 estimates.

By February 1945 Warsaw was a capital city again, but not of a free nation. The Soviets had taken over and established the Communist Polish People's Republic.

*King Sigismund's Column, which honors the ruler who relocated Poland's capital from Kraków to Warsaw in 1596, stands in the middle of Zamkowy Square in Warsaw.* (Courtesy Polish National Tourist Office)

To understand Warsaw, you must know its two sections, divided by the Vistula. To the east, on the left bank, are modern residential neighborhoods where most of the people live. To the west, on the right bank, is the bustling downtown just north of which is Warsaw's celebrated Old Town (Stare Miasto), which dates back to the 13th century. Its ancient buildings, twisting medieval streets, and grand churches have been lovingly restored. To add to the charm of this medieval "town," the government has closed it off to motorized traffic. Couples stroll its streets on foot or in horse-drawn carriages. The Old Town marketplace is alive with outdoor art displays and cozy cafés called *karviarnie*, where students, artists, and writers sit and sip coffee, eat cake, and talk.

Nearby is the Royal Walk, a two-mile (3 km) route that stretches from Castle Square, site of Warsaw's Royal Castle, once the abode of Polish kings and presidents, to Lazienki Palace, whose park houses a monument to Poland's greatest composer, Frédéric Chopin. Concerts of Chopin's music are held in the park each summer, while every five years the city hosts the Chopin International Piano Competition. Chopin's home is another highlight on the Royal Walk. So are the Laboratory of Physical Sciences where Madame Curie once worked, the University of Warsaw, and the Botanical Gardens.

The new Warsaw, however, is not as comforting as the old. And it presents stark and disturbing contrasts to visitors, as this Polish-American writer observed:

> Stretch limousines carry the new rich through the streets. Ikea, the Swedish furniture chain, and Benetton, the Italian apparel outfit, have opened stores to sell them merchandise. . . . But while people earning $60 a week can buy books and, from time to time, a Benetton sweater for $30 . . . they can't afford much more. . . .
>
> Most Poles still live in run-down buildings whose piping breaks down regularly. Windowpanes in the doors of apartment buildings are broken, half covered with cardboard. This is not in slum territories but in respectable middle-class neighborhoods.

Crime and cars are two other problems that plague postcommunist Warsaw as it enters the 21st century. The city has become a stop on European drug-smuggling routes, and gangs and the Mafia have turned it at times into a battleground between criminals and the police.

Warsaw's worn-out roadways are ill equipped to deal with the more than 4 million motor vehicles that clog them daily. Reckless and drunk drivers have resulted in a steady increase in auto accidents, injuries, and fatalities. Air pollution from unrestricted car emissions is also a pressing problem.

## Legendary Kraków

In 1995 Kraków (population 733,100), Poland's third largest city, was named one of nine European Cities of Culture for the new millennium, setting off a five-year celebration of musical, artistic, literary, and theatrical events. Its selection was no surprise to the people of Kraków.

If Warsaw is Poland's Moscow, then Kraków is surely its St. Petersburg. Kraków emerged from the catastrophe of World War II practically unscathed. Its age-old beauty entranced even the cold-hearted German Nazi commanders who decided to make it their headquarters. Thus its magnificent castles and cathedrals were spared the devastation of war.

Kraków was a thriving trade center when Warsaw was still a village. Here is how author Eric P. Kelly describes 15th-century Kraków in his historical novel *The Trumpeter of Krakow,* as seen through the eyes of a Polish family entering the city for the first time:

> All about them rose in the bright sunlit palaces, churches, towers, battlement walls, and Gothic buildings, as yet for the most part unadorned by the rich sculpture that was to come in a few years under the influence of the Italian Renaissance. . . .
>
> Here for the moment in this great international capital of East and West was worshiped every god that man knows, it might even be said that God himself was worshiped under many names and in many languages and dialects. Here was Turks, Cossacks, Ruthenians, Germans, Flemings, Czechs, and Slovaks, with their wares to sell, and Hungarians with their wines from the mellow plains of Transylvania.

A very different view of Kraków in the 1990s, emerging from 40 years of Communist neglect, is offered by U.S. correspondent for the *New York Times* Jane Perlez:

> Cracow . . . is emerging again as a European city of charm and vibrancy. Many of the elegant small Gothic and Renaissance palaces that rim the main square have been repainted in the last two years. Jazz spots in stone cellars are being scrubbed down; new sidewalk cafés with spiffy furniture and umbrellas are opening almost weekly, it seems. . . .
>
> This reawakening is taking place against the backdrop of Cracow's immutable strengths: an old town of narrow cobbled streets and 60 churches . . .

Perhaps the most prominent of these "strengths" is Wawel Hill, a natural limestone promontory that overlooks the banks of the Vistula in south-central Poland. On it sits Wawel Royal Castle and Wawel Cathedral. Legend has it, before either of these were built, there was a cave on the site, inhabited by a terrible dragon. The Wawel Dragon was the terror of the Polish countryside, burning homes and eating people and animals.

The king of the region offered a tempting reward to any knight who could slay the creature—the hand of his daughter in marriage and his kingdom to rule after his death. Many brave knights tried to vanquish the dragon, but all died in the attempt.

A shoemaker's apprentice named Krak decided to use his wits to defeat the monster. Krak stuffed a ram's skin with sulfur, sewed it up, and placed it before the dragon's cave. The hungry beast devoured the skin, and the sulfur caused the flame in its stomach to burn all the more intensely. The dragon became extremely thirsty and quaffed down water from the river until he was ready to burst. Krak began to tease the dragon, whose fire was quenched by the water and could now spew out only steam. The frustrated dragon puffed out more and more steam, until the pressure of the steam in his body caused him to explode. Krak won the princess and celebrated his good future by building a castle on top of the dragon's cave. He called it Wawel castle after the unfortunate dragon and founded the city of Kraków, which grew up around the castle.

Wawel Cathedral is more firmly grounded in Polish history. It was built by Bolesław the Brave in 1020 and later became the burial place of Polish kings and such national heroes as Tadeusz Kościuszko and Józef Piłsudski. Here also lies the silver tomb of St. Stanisław (Stanislaus), Poland's patron saint.

Bolesław's successors made Kraków the capital of Poland in 1038, and it remained so for more than 500 years. The crown jewel of Poland's "golden age," Kraków is home to the nation's oldest university, the University of Kraków (now Jagiellonian University), built in 1364 by Casimir the Great and designed by Italian Renaissance architects. Among the most precious articles on display at the university are the astronomical tools of Copernicus, who studied there, and the world-famous Jagiellonian Globe, made in 1510 and the first to show the New World lands.

Another beguiling legend, this one based on fact, is connected with the Church of St. Mary. Seven hundred years ago the people of Kraków were celebrating in the church, when a watchman in the church tower saw an invading army of Tatars advancing in a surprise attack. The watchman immediately lifted his trumpet and played the "Heynal," a hymn to the Virgin Mary and a signal of alarm. An approaching Tatar soldier shot the watchman in the throat with an arrow. The brave trumpeter died, having alerted the people of Kraków to the danger and thereby saving the city from destruction. In remembrance of this historical moment, a trumpeter plays the "Heynal" in the same church tower every hour of the day. When he comes to the high note, he breaks off, just as the original trumpeter did when pierced by the arrow.

One local landmark found just outside Kraków lies far beneath the Earth's surface. The remarkable salt-mining town of Wieliczka has been in operation at least since the 13th century. Its nine levels reach a depth of more than 984 feet (300 m). Visitors can take a fascinating 90-minute tour of the mines by elevator. They view underground chapels that house huge statues, altar rails, and chandeliers carved from rock salt by the miners themselves. Other chambers contain a museum, a ballroom, and even a tennis court for the miners. There is a more serious side to

Wieliczka as well. Asthma patients find they can breathe more easily in the salt-laden air of the mine. They are treated for their illness in a special sanatorium.

A more prosaic but vitally important part of Kraków's economy is Nowa Huta (literally, "New Foundry"), Poland's largest steel mill, built by the Communists after World War II. In 1996 Nowa Huta produced 7.5 million tons of steel, a third of the total Polish steel production. The mill has brought both prosperity and problems to Kraków. Its poisonous fumes, along with those of the coal-fueled plants nearby, have created air pollution that is damaging the city's ancient buildings as well as posing a health hazard to its people.

## Gdańsk—Birthplace of Polish Freedom

Far to the north lies Poland's largest port city, Gdańsk (population 456,700; 2003 estimate). Gdańsk is one of Poland's newer cities, although it has a long and turbulent past. A Slavic settlement around the year 1000, Gdańsk was taken over by the Teutonic Knights in 1308. The Poles and Knights struggled for control of the port for more than a century. Poland finally won it in 1466. It was renamed Danzig in 1793, when it became a Prussian port on the North Sea during the second partition, and remained so until 1919. It is the birthplace of such celebrated Germans as philosopher Arthur Schopenhauer (1788–1860) and writer Günter Grass (b. 1927). It was returned to Poland in the Treaty of Versailles following World War I. The retaking of Gdańsk by the Germans in 1939 sparked World War II. The city was returned to the Poles in May 1945 by the invading Russians: The Germans were expelled from Danzig, and the city rechristened Gdańsk. The city was famous again in 1980 when the trade union Solidarity was formed there by Lech Wałesa and others.

Poland's most important port on the Baltic Sea, Gdańsk has some of the largest shipyards in the world. The city's largest, owned by the state, nearly shut down in 1996 but was then sold in 1998. Currently, shipbuilding is still being done in Gdańsk but on a smaller scale. Gdańsk is also a center for the metallurgical and chemical industries, sawmilling, and brewing and distilling. Among Gdańsk's historical buildings are the

*The people of Gdańsk stroll along a waterfront avenue. The city has traditionally made its living from the sea in shipbuilding, fishing, and trading.* (Courtesy Kari Ann Butler)

Gothic Church of St. Mary built in 1343 and one of the largest Protestant churches in the world.

# Ancient Poznań and Gniezno

Older than Kraków, the city of Poznań (population 581,200) is the first fortified settlement built by the Polanie in the 800s and later home of the Piast kings. Like Gdańsk, this city was taken over by the Prussians in 1793 and returned to Poland in 1919. Once a major trading center, Poznań revived its traditional spring fair day in 1922 as the International Trade Fair where capitalist and communist countries could trade peacefully. Among Poznań's many historical landmarks is the Gold Chapel, where the tombs of Mieszko I and his son Bolesław the Brave reside.

Oldest of all Polish cities, Gniezno celebrated the 1,000th anniversary of the death of its patron saint, St. Adalbertus, in 1997. It was the first capital of the Polish kingdom, the place where kings were crowned until 1320, and the site where Christianity was first established in what is now Poland. Once a rural town of farmers, present-day Gniezno boasts a tannery, factories that produce shoes and other products, and engineering plants. It is home to a museum that includes relics of the first Piast kings, a beautiful 14th-century cathedral, and a modern auto race track.

## Cultural Lublin and Wrocław

Lovely Lublin (population 354,200) in southeastern Poland is home to five universities, including Catholic University, which was renamed the Maria Curie-Skłodowska University in 1944 in honor of Poland's greatest scientist. Lublin has played a critical role in Polish history. The legislative assemblies that united Poland and Lithuania in 1569 were held here. In 1918 Lublin was the seat of the temporary Polish Socialist government, and in 1944 it was the seat of the provisional government that stood opposed to the Polish government-in-exile in London. Today Lublin is a manufacturing center as well as an educational one. Textiles, electrical products, agricultural machinery, and automobiles are made here.

Halfway between Poznań and Kraków in southwest Poland lies the City of Bridges, Wrocław (population 632,200). Some 84 bridges cross the Oder River in this quaint city, home to about 40,000 students at numerous colleges and the University of Wrocław, founded in 1811. In Wrocław also reside two of Poland's most distinguished theater companies—the Jerzy Grotowski Theatre Laboratory and the Henryk Tomaszewski Pantomime Theater. The city is a river port and a manufacturing center, where textiles, machinery, iron goods, and railroad equipment are made.

Poland's cities have survived wars and invasions and have emerged triumphantly. They are living symbols of the perseverance and indomitable spirit of the Polish people.

## NOTES

p. 102 "'Stretch limousines carry the new rich . . .'" Katarzyna Wandycz, "The Polish Zoo," *Forbes*, May 25, 1992, p. 134.

p. 103 "'All about them rose . . .'" Eric P. Kelly. *The Trumpeter of Krakow* (New York: Macmillan, 1966), pp. 18–19.

p. 104 "'Cracow . . . is emerging again . . .'" Jane Perlez, "Cracow Emerges from the Shadows," *New York Times*, July 18, 1993, p. 14.

# 10

# PRESENT PROBLEMS AND FUTURE SOLUTIONS

Before looking at the problems facing this nation in transition, it might do well to look at what is right with Poland. Unlike some of its neighbors, such as the countries that made up the former Yugoslavia and Czechoslovakia, Poland is not troubled by ethnic divisiveness. Its generally well-educated, hard-working populace shares a common ancestry and traditions that help it pull together for change, despite differences of opinion. Even Poland's geography, long a curse, may finally, in postcommunist Europe, prove a blessing. Its central location between a non-threatening, reunited Germany and a Russia that has divested itself of its Soviet empire, may help it prosper both politically and economically.

Strong political and economic ties to the United States bode well for Poland's future. Its expected accession into the European Union (EU) in 2004 will strengthen bonds with its neighbors and further stimulate a lagging economy.

This is the good news. Now for the problems and some possible solutions.

## Unemployment

In January 2002 the unemployment rate in Poland hit a new postcommunist high of 18 percent. Some 3.3 million Poles were out of work. The

*Young Poles celebrate the official results of the EU accession referendum in Warsaw on June 8, 2003. Poland, along with nine other nations, will be given full membership in the European trade bloc in spring 2004.* (AP Photo/Alik Keplicz)

rate is expected to climb higher as an estimated 1 million new school graduates were expected to enter the job market that year.

Why is unemployment so high? Obviously a strong downturn in the economy since 2000 is a major factor. Also, the continuing sell-off or downsizing of large, inefficient state-run industries has caused many workers to lose their jobs.

While joining the EU is seen as a major solution to the unemployment problem, some EU member nations are fearful that, after Poland becomes a member, Polish workers will migrate for work and hurt their own fragile job markets. EU members Germany and Austria are calling for a seven-year transitional period before workers from a new EU member state can find work in another EU country. "In seven years time the unemployment rate will still be very high, and may well be around 20 percent," predicted Robert Beenj of the investment bank Lehman Brothers, "so in the short term the problem [for the EU] will be avoided but it won't go away."

# Business Growth and Corruption

In many ways the Poles are in a better position to adapt to capitalism than their eastern European neighbors. The Communists allowed more private businesses and farms to operate here than anywhere else behind the Iron Curtain. From July 1990 to June 30, 1997, the privatization process was begun in 4,100 state-run companies. By mid-1997, 1,351 state-owned companies were completely in private hands, and 635 state companies that were inefficient were liquidated. As of that date there were still 3,326 state-owned businesses left in Poland.

Despite these advancements, the Poles do not have the experience or skill to run their businesses as effectively as they could. Foreign investment and U.S. corporations have been accelerating their involvement. In October 2003 the Outlet Company of Great Britain opened only the second factory outlet in Poland in Sosnowiec. Within five years the company plans to build more outlets in such cities as Gdańsk, Poznań, and Szczecin. About the same time the Ireland-based Dyanair airline became the first competition to the national air carrier LOT Polish Airlines, and other foreign airlines are expected to follow. LOT is cutting costs to improve service and better compete with other carriers, a winning formula for consumers.

Meanwhile, despite economic problems, new businesses continue to grow in number. A new generation of young Poles has embraced capitalism. Many have lost the idealistic mindset of their parents and grandparents, who struggled against a communist system, and are more materialistic and competitive. "This generation is not interested in ideological issues and they are not post-materialist," noted Professor Mirosława Grabowska of the Warsaw University Institute of Sociology. "They are very interested in money and career."

This chase after wealth has led to a failure in morality in some cases. Bribery and corruption in business are common and now extend to the halls of government itself. In February 2003 government investigative hearings were held in the so-called Rywingate scandal. Lew Rywin, a leading Polish film producer who coproduced the 2002 Oscar-winning movie *The Pianist*, has been accused of asking for a $17.5 million bribe from the editor of Poland's leading newspaper *Gazeta Wyborcza*. In return, Rywin allegedly would have secured amendments to enable the paper's parent company, Agora, to buy a private television station, prohibited by existing Polish law. What made the incident a national scandal was that Rywin claimed to be the representative of Prime Minister Leszek Miller. While Miller has vehemently denied knowledge of the bribe, public Polish Television (TVP) president Robert Kwiatkowski was also implicated and removed from his post. The Miller government's promise to end corruption must be backed by swift action if it is to earn the trust of the Polish people.

# Crime

Along with corruption, crime has been on the upswing in postcommunist Poland, as it has been in Russia and other eastern European countries, where tight Soviet control once discouraged criminal activity. Crime has become highly organized, has the support of corrupt police, and is increasingly violent. Drug smuggling, prostitution, protection rackets, and murder for hire are now common in many cities.

In March 2003 one policeman was killed and 15 injured in a shootout in a Warsaw suburb with two fugitive smugglers, who held them off for 10 hours with automatic rifles, grenades, and homemade nail bombs before they were killed. Some of the growing number of criminals in Poland are homegrown, but others are part of the mafia of Russia, Turkey, and Italy. Leading Italian mafioso Francesco O was using Polish banks to send money to the accounts of members of the Sicilian Mafia before he was arrested by the Central Investigating Bureau in 2003.

Equally disturbing is the growth of criminal behavior among Polish youth. Large, sterile housing projects in major cities, where unemployment runs rampant, have become breeding grounds for petty crime and drug addiction among young men. Some of these angry youth have found an alternative to crime in the creative expression of hip-hop music.

"It's absolutely sure that if I wasn't rapping, I'd be stealing," said leading Polish hip-hop artist Peja. "A lot of people think Polish hip-hop is only about the street, but we are talking about ourselves, our relationships, other problems." However, while music is cathartic in expressing their despair, for most of these neglected youth it is not a long-term solution to the problems of crime and urban squalor.

Polish leaders are doing their best to cope with the situation and have sought the help of more experienced law enforcement agencies in the West. For example, the U.S. Federal Bureau of Investigation (FBI) has opened an office in Warsaw to combat the infiltration of the Russian mafia in Poland's capital.

# The Environment

Poland's natural environment—its air, water, land, and forests—are under serious assault from pollution. The threat to the environment is part the grim legacy of communism and part the bitter fruit of newly transplanted capitalism. The steel furnaces built by the Soviets at Nowa Huta are hopelessly antiquated and continue to emit deadly clouds of carbon monoxide and sulfur dioxide that blanket the city of Kraków. The sulfur, 250 percent above safety limits, eats away at the city's venerable, old sandstone buildings. Pollution control equipment installed by the U.S. Department of Energy has partially alleviated the problem, but until the furnaces are replaced, this modern dragon of Kraków will not be vanquished.

A major solution to the widespread pollution is the shutting down of Soviet-era factories, which was begun in the mid-1990s. As Poland relies less and less on heavy industry for its economy, the situation is slowly but steadily improving.

Western prosperity, however, has brought new environmental problems with it. Capitalism has put more than 5 million private cars on Poland's roadways, increasing air pollution and causing traffic jams in large cities. Emissions regulations for new cars are lax, and unleaded gas is not yet mandatory. Western-style fast-food restaurants and other new businesses are turning Poles into greater consumers, and the increase in disposable garbage, often sitting uncollected in cities for weeks, is alarming.

Some of Poland's environmental problems have their source outside the country's borders. The so-called Black Triangle, a plateau Poland shares with the Czech Republic and Germany, produces some of the worst acid rain in the world. The sulfur and soot from nearby coal-burning power plants mix with rain to destroy healthy forests. More than half of

Poland's conifers and deciduous trees have lost over a quarter of their needles and leaves due to acid rain. As the trees die off, soil erosion will worsen, creating serious spring flooding.

## A POLISH FAMILY IN AMERICA

The great migration from Poland that my grandparents were a part of did not begin in the 20th century but goes back to the very beginnings of America. One of the first emigrant ships arriving in Jamestown in October 1608 included a group of Polish artisans, recruited to help establish the economic base of the tiny colony in present-day Virginia. They helped build a glassworks, which may have been the first factory in America.

Between 1900 and 1914 more Poles came to the United States than ever before. They were among the four largest groups of immigrants in the great wave of European immigration. Many of them settled in the new industrial cities of the Midwest—Milwaukee, Chicago, Detroit, and Cleveland—where they worked in factories, slaughterhouses, and mines.

Polish political refugees from communism began coming to the United States in the late 1940s and continued until the declaration of martial law in the early 1980s, when ordinary citizens were forbidden to leave Poland. Since the collapse of communism in 1989, some Poles abroad have returned home, but many more have chosen to stay in their new homelands.

Not all the new immigrants have come for political reasons. Typical of this group are the Pierzak family of Stratford, Connecticut. Teresa Pierzak is a registered nurse who came to the United States in 1976, when she was 23 years old, to find a better life with more opportunity. Her grandparents and her father had lived in the United States but returned to Poland later in life. Teresa, however, came to stay.

"When I first got here, I couldn't believe how much money I was paid," she recalls. "I thought to myself, 'How will I ever spend so much money?'" She met her husband, Janusz, through mutual friends. A Polish toolmaker, he arrived in the United States five years before Teresa.

The Pierzaks have stayed close to their Polish roots. Many of their friends are Polish, and they belong to a nearby Polish social club. Janusz reads mainly Polish-language newspapers and magazines. They have introduced their two children, Robert and Sylvia, to Polish traditions and culture and have visited Poland as a family five times.

Although more and more Poles are concerned about what pollution is doing to their country, the need for economic growth has so far outstripped any concern for the environment. Until the economy fully

Robert attends Ithaca College, in upstate New York, where he majors in music composition. A gifted pianist and composer, he won the prestigious BMI (Broadcast Music Incorporated) Student Composer Award for 2003. While he considers himself an American first, Robert appreciates his Polish heritage. "I'm thankful that I have an ingrained European way of thinking and looking at things in this country," he says.

His sister, Sylvia, is an honor student at high school and a member of the track team. She also speaks and reads Polish and belongs to a Polish folk-dancing group. "Many kids I know in school have no sense of culture, no sense of respect," Sylvia says. "My friends don't know anything about their ethnic heritage, and I do. I feel I have a broader outlook on things."

Today, an estimated 7 to 15 million people of Polish descent live in the United States, the largest population outside Poland. Chicago, the city with the largest Polish-American population—more than a million—has more Poles than any city except Warsaw.

*The Pierzaks, a Polish-American family living in Stratford, Connecticut, are (from left to right) Teresa, Robert, Sylvia, and Janusz. (Courtesy Janusz Pierzak)*

recovers, Poland, like many other countries in eastern Europe, will probably not turn its full attention to cleaning up the air, water, and land.

# Education and Illiteracy

Although education is nearly universal, 70 percent of Poles have only a
primary school education and only six out of 100 people have been to a
university. According to research done at Poznań University, 30 percent
of the population is functionally illiterate. Even more disturbing, nearly
three-quarters of the people do not understand much of what they read
and hear in the media. This is a bad constituency for a new democracy
where people need to be prepared to make informed decisions based on
the changing events going on around them. While the government is
making some efforts to improve education, new funds will have to be
found to make the educational system meet the needs of more of the
population.

# The Role of the Church

In the 40 years of communist Poland the Roman Catholic Church played
a dominant role in Polish life. It kept hope alive for millions of Poles. In
postcommunist Poland, the church's attempts to control Polish society
are resented by millions of Catholic Poles. The church's support of anti-
abortion legislation and the efforts of priests to influence who their
parishioners vote for have caused the church to slip in public opinion
polls. And yet most Catholics are still unified behind their pope.

In August 2002, in a farewell address to the people of Kraków that
ended a four-day visit to his homeland, the pope warned his countrymen
and women not to abandon their faith in an increasingly secular world.
"When the noisy propaganda of liberalism, of freedom without truth or
responsibility, grows stronger in our country, too," he said, "the shepherds
of the church cannot fail to proclaim the one fail-proof philosophy of
freedom, which is the truth of the cross of Christ." That truth will continue to wield great power in Poland, although the earthly church and its
representatives continue to be questioned.

# Health and Health Care

A naturally robust people, the Poles face serious health issues in the 21st century. Air pollution from widespread coal-burning plants has led to high rates of such respiratory diseases as emphysema, tuberculosis, and asthma. Birth defects, stillborn children, and low birth rates are other tragic results of growing air and water pollution, especially in the Katowice region. The government must increase expenditures on public health to combat these problems.

Other health problems are self-inflicted and reflect the high level of anxiety of a nation in transition. Alcoholism, drug abuse, and suicide are growing problems among a workforce that is facing high unemployment and an uncertain future.

In addition, Poles are the world's heaviest smokers, according to the World Health Organization (WHO). In 1999, 25 percent of all Poles smoked, and 70,000 people die each year from smoking-related illnesses. The cause of death of half of all Polish men who die before age 65 is lung cancer.

The government has begun to take a strong stand against smoking. In 1999 President Aleksander Kwaśniewski signed a bill banning all tobacco ads and tobacco company sponsorships of sporting and cultural events by 2001. The antismoking campaign is beginning to produce results, despite recent efforts of North American tobacco companies to market more aggressively their cigarettes in eastern Europe as their home markets go into decline. "The law itself will not change much," admitted Polish Health Ministry spokesman Tadeusz Parchimowicz, "but the law helps others to change attitude."

The Polish health care system under the Soviets began to fall apart in the 1970s and 1980s from inefficiency, corruption, and shortages. When communism fell, the new democratic government saw the health care system as so problematic that it left it virtually untouched for a decade. Finally in 1999 the problems of health care could be ignored no longer. A new privatized system was devised based on health insurance. The Health Insurance Act of 1999 passed by the Sejm requires every citizen to pay 7.5 percent of his or her income tax to a central health insurance institution called Kasa Chorych.

While the new system is superior to the old government-run one, it has its problems. Hospitals and health care centers are still underfunded and often in desperate need of updating and repair. Medical staff continue to be poorly paid and often are in conflict with management. Insurance premiums, some say, are too low to fund the best care.

Despite these problems, primary health care has definitely improved, and privatization has made care more effective, stable, and thorough. As the national health care system works out the bugs and stabilizes itself, more Poles will get the kind of health care that they deserve.

Perhaps the biggest problem facing Poland today is more psychological than political, geographical, or economic. There is a strange malaise that has overtaken the nation since the first heady days of freedom after communism's fall. Disillusionment over former heroes such as Lech Wałesa and leaders of the Catholic Church has made Poles, as a group, somewhat cautious and skeptical about the future. The election of former Communists to power shows that the Poles are not yet ready to close the door on the past for an unknown and untested future. This reaction is not as dangerous as it might be in Russia or some other eastern European countries. The Poles, with a long tradition of democracy, do not have to overcome, for example, the czarist past of Russia, which has known little but autocratic rule in its history.

The autocrats who ruled Poland were usually invaders and conquerors. They may have conquered the Polish land but never the soul of its people. It is this indomitable spirit that is Poland's best hope for the future, a future that promises to be perhaps this courageous and remarkable country's greatest golden age yet. In that sense Poland is a model for other nations making the same difficult transition from communism to a more democratic system.

As one writer puts it, much more may hinge on Poland's successful transition to democracy than the fate of one nation:

Poland is the vestibule [passageway] to the 21st century. If the current experiment in liberty succeeds in Poland, and if prosperity spreads throughout the land, then the prospects for liberty and prosperity in Belarus [a former republic of the Soviet Union] and in neighboring Ukraine improve considerably; and then so do those of Russia—and on eastward to China. Contrarily, if Poland fails, then the failure of the others is virtually foredoomed and the 21st century could become more tyrannous and bloody than the 20th.

These are words worth heeding for all of us who value liberty and freedom.

## NOTES

p. 112 "'In seven years time . . .'" BBC News. Available on-line. URL: http://news.bbc.co.uk/1/low/business/1834336.stm. Downloaded March 26, 2003.

p. 113 "'This generation is not interested . . .'" *New York Times*, January 1, 1998, p. A1.

p. 114 "'It's absolutely sure that . . .'" *New York Times*, April 5, 2002, p. A4.

p. 116 "'When I first got here . . .'" Teresa Pierzak, in an interview with the author, 1995.

p. 117 "'I'm thankful that I have . . .'" Robert Pierzak, in an interview with the author, April 27, 2003.

p. 117 "'Many kids I know . . .'" Sylvia Pierzak, in an interview with the author, April 27, 2003.

p. 118 "'When the noisy propaganda of liberalism . . .'" "Pope's sad farewell to Poland." Polonia Global Fund website. Available online. URL: www.pgf.cc/religion/pope-poland2002.htm. Downloaded August 28, 2003.

p. 119 "'The law itself will not . . .'" Kitty McKinsey. "Poland: Anti-Smoking Campaign Targets World's Heaviest Smokers." Radio Free Europe. Available online. URL:http://www.rferl.org.nca/features/1997/05/F.RU.97052090608.html. Downloaded March 27, 2003.

pp. 120–121 "'Poland is the vestibule . . .'" Michael Novak, "Don't Abandon Us!" *Forbes*, January 17, 1994, p. 51.

# CHRONOLOGY

### 800s
The Polanie unite the Slavic tribes

### 966
The Poles adopt Christianity under Mieszko I

### 1025
Bolesław I is crowned first king of Poland

### 1364
Casimir the Great founds the University of Kraków

### 1386
Lithuania and Poland are united in the marriage of Queen Jadwiga and Grand Duke Władysław Jagiełło

### 1410
Władysław II Jagiełło leads the Poles to victory over the Teutonic Knights at the Battle of Grünwald; Poland's Golden Age begins

### 1493
Poland's first national parliament is established

### 1587
The Jagiellonian dynasty ends, along with the Golden Age

## 1596

King Sigismund III Vasa moves the capital from Kraków to Warsaw

## 1683

John Sobieski defeats the Turks at the Battle of Vienna

## 1735

The two-year War of the Polish Succession ends in defeat for the descendants of Sobieski and victory for German Saxony

## 1772

Poland is partitioned by Austria, Prussia, and Russia

## 1793

The Second Partition is enacted by Prussia and Russia

## 1794

Tadeusz Kościuszko's uprising is defeated

## 1795

The Third Partition of Poland ends its existence as an independent state

## 1807

Napoléon creates the Duchy of Warsaw, briefly returning Poland to the map of Europe

## 1830

The first 19th-century uprising against the Russians begins in Warsaw

## 1863

The second Warsaw uprising ends in defeat for the Poles

## 1914

World War I begins; the Poles, under Józef Piłsudski, fight against the Russians on the Austrian side

## 1919

The Treaty of Versailles returns Poland to the status of an independent nation

## 1921

Russia returns some Polish territory under the Treaty of Riga

## 1923

Piłsudski resigns as premier

## 1926

Piłsudski becomes dictator in a bloodless military coup

## 1939

Poland is invaded by Germany and then Russia, setting off World War II

## 1943

Jews in the Warsaw Ghetto rise up against the Nazis in a month of fighting

## 1944

Another uprising in Warsaw devastates the city as the Germans prepare to withdraw in World War II's last days

## 1945

Soviet Communists begin to take over the government of Poland

## 1948

The Soviets clamp down; Polish Communist Party leader Władysław Gomułka is forced to resign

## 1952

Stefan Cardinal Wyszyński is imprisoned

## 1956

Antigovernment demonstrations and riots in Poznań and other cities lead to some reforms and the return of Gomułka to power

## 1968

Student strikes and protests against the government at the University of
Warsaw and elsewhere lead to the firing of numerous teachers, many
of whom leave the country

## 1970

*December 15:* On "Bloody Tuesday," 55 workers in Gdańsk are killed by
police in "bread riots" that lead to the burning of the city's Communist Party headquarters
*December 20:* Edward Gierek replaces Gomułka as Communist Party
leader

## 1978

Karol Cardinal Wojtyla, archbishop of Kraków, is elected pope of the
Roman Catholic Church and becomes John Paul II

## 1980

*August 31:* An organization of Gdańsk workers is recognized by the government as a free union, and workers win the right to strike
*September:* Gierek is replaced as party leader by Stanisław Kania
*November 10:* The government recognizes Solidarity, a grouping of 36
independent unions, by granting it a charter
*December:* Rural Solidarity, a trade organization for farmers, is founded
in Warsaw

## 1981

*September:* Solidarity's first National Congress of Delegates convenes in
Gdańsk
*October:* Kania is replaced by General Wojciech Jaruzelski
*December 13:* Jaruzelski declares martial law, and Solidarity's activities
are suspended

## 1982

*October:* Solidarity is officially outlawed; Lech Wałesa wins the Nobel
Peace Prize

## 1983

*June:* Pope John Paul II visits Poland for the third time and acts as a mediator between Solidarity and the government

## 1984

*October:* Father Jerzy Popieluszko, a Solidarity priest, is murdered by secret police, setting off a national protest

## 1985

Mikhail Gorbachev becomes the new leader of the Soviet Union and soon begins far-reaching reforms

## 1987

Price increases of up to 100 percent on goods and services are announced

## 1989

*February:* Roundtable discussions begin between the government and Solidarity leaders

*April:* The two sides sign accords legalizing Solidarity and preparing the way for free elections

*June 4:* In the first free elections since the end of World War II, Solidarity wins 99 of 100 seats in the new senate

*July 4:* The new Polish parliament convenes

*November:* Wałesa visits the United States and addresses a joint meeting of Congress

## 1990

*January:* The Communist Party of Poland votes to disband itself; Prime Minister Tadeusz Mazowiecki declares a program of radical economic reform

*September:* Jaruzelski resigns as president, and new presidential elections are scheduled

*December:* Wałesa becomes the first popularly elected president in 50 years

## 1991

**October:** The first fully free parliamentary election brings 29 political parties into parliament

## 1992

**June:** Wałesa's first coalition government falls apart; Hanna Suchocka becomes the first female prime minister in eastern Europe in the 20th century as her Democratic Union Party wins in new elections

## 1993

**April:** The lower house approves a privatization plan for state-owned industry

**September:** The Democratic Left Alliance, made up of former Communists, ousts the Democratic Union from power

**October:** Waldemar Pawlak, leader of the Polish Peasant Party (PSL), becomes the sixth prime minister since the fall of communism

## 1994

**January:** The North Atlantic Treaty Organization (NATO) announces that Poland and other eastern European countries are invited to be part of its newly formed Partnership for Peace

**June:** The first military exercises of 13 countries representing Partnership for Peace are held in Poland

**August:** Two Polish generals are acquitted of involvement in the murder of Father Popieluszko over the protests of the people

**September:** The Official State Secrets Act, a blow for many to democratic reforms, passes in the lower house of parliament

## 1995

**February:** Józef Oleksy, a senior member of the Democratic Left Alliance, becomes prime minister, replacing Pawlak

**December:** Former Communist minister Aleksander Kwaśniewski narrowly defeats Wałesa in the presidential election

## 1996

**October:** Poet Wisława Szymborska wins the Nobel Prize in Literature

## 1997

*September:* Solidarity makes a strong comeback in parliamentary elections and forms a new coalition government with the Freedom Union (FU)

## 1998

Parliament passes the Health Insurance Act to improve and widen national health care

## 1999

*March:* Poland, along with the Czech Republic and Hungary, is admitted as a full member of NATO

## 2000

*October:* Kwaśniewski is reelected president for a second five-year term

## 2001

*June:* U.S. president George W. Bush visits Poland; the parliament passes the Education Act to improve the education system

*October:* Leszek Miller, chairman of the Democratic Left Alliance (SLD), is appointed prime minister

## 2002

*January:* Russian president Vladimir Putin visits Poland; the national unemployment rate hits a new high of 18 percent

*July:* President Kwaśniewski visits the United States

*August:* Pope John Paul II makes his ninth papal visit to his native Poland

*December:* The European Union (EU) formally approves membership for Poland and nine other countries to take effect in May 2004

## 2003

*March:* Prime Minister Miller drops the PSL from the coalition government on charges of political blackmail; government hearings begin on the Rywingate scandal involving possible bribery and corruption in the government; coalition forces, including 200 Polish soldiers, attack Iraq and within a month bring down the government of dictator

Saddam Hussein; Polish-born film director Roman Polanski wins the Academy Award for best director for his motion picture *The Pianist*, which he filmed in Poland

**April:** Poland agrees to buy 48 U.S.-made F16 jet fighters to help upgrade its air force

**June 7–8:** Poles vote overwhelmingly in favor of joining the EU in a national referendum

# FURTHER READING

## NONFICTION

Ascherson, Neal. *The Struggles for Poland.* New York: Random House, 1987. A concise adult history of Poland in the 20th century through the mid-1980s.

Ash, Timothy Garton. *The Polish Revolution: Solidarity.* New Haven, Conn.: Yale University Press, 2002. A vivid account of the Solidarity movement from 1980.

Davies, Norman. *God's Playground: A History of Poland,* 2 vols. New York: Columbia University Press, 1982. A monumental study of Polish history from its beginnings to the last decade of communism. Written for adults.

Donica, Ewa, and Tim Sharman. *We Live in Poland.* New York: Bookwright Press, 1985. Part of a fascinating young adult series that views Poland through interviews with individuals in representative roles and careers.

Gwertzman, Bernard, and Michael T. Kaufman, eds. *The Collapse of Communism.* New York: Times Books, 1990. A blow-by-blow chronological account from the pages of the *New York Times* of events in Poland, the Soviet Union, and other countries in Eastern Europe during the critical years 1989–90.

Hintz, Martin. *Poland.* Chicago: Children's Press, 1998. An excellent well-illustrated introduction for young adults to Polish history and culture, part of the Enchantment of the World series.

Madison, Arnold. *Polish Greats.* New York: David McKay Co., 1980. Short biographies of such famous Poles as Copernicus, Kościuszko, Chopin, and John Paul II. Young adult.

Michener, James. *Pilgrimage: A Memoir of Poland and Rome.* Emmaus, Pa.: Rodale Press, 1990. Thoughts and observations from this leading American novelist during a 1988 trip to Poland and the Vatican to visit with Pope John Paul.

Snyder, Timothy. *The Reconstruction of Nations: Poland, Ukraine, Lithuania, Belarus, 1569–1999.* New Haven, Conn.: Yale University Press, 2003. A fine critical study of the history of nationhood in eastern Europe, focusing on Poland.

Zamoyski, Adam. *The Polish Way: A Thousand-Year History of the Poles and Their Culture.* New York: Hippocrene Books, 1993. An excellent introductory history written by a member of a historically famous Polish family.

## FICTION

Borowski, Tadeusz. *This Way for the Gas, Ladies and Gentlemen*. New York: Penguin, 1976. Gripping stories about everyday life in the Polish concentration camps of World War II by a Polish writer who lived through the nightmare.

Kelly, Eric P. *The Trumpeter of Krakow*. New York: Macmillan, 1966. A Newberry Award–winning novel for young adults about a family in 15th-century Kraków. An outstanding historical novel, first published in 1928.

Michener, James. *Poland*. New York: Fawcett Crest, 1984. An epic journey through Polish history tracing the fortunes of three families by an American master of the historical novel.

Mrozek, Sławomir. *The Elephant*. New York: Grove Press, 1965. Short, satirical, fablelike stories by a leading contemporary Polish writer that mock the bureaucratic soullessness of the Communist government and the people living under it.

Sienkiewicz, Henryk. *With Fire and Sword*. New York: Hippocrene Books, 1991. The last volume in this Nobel Prize–winning Polish novelist's trilogy about turbulent 17th-century Poland.

Szymborska, Wisława. *Poems New and Collected*. San Diego, Calif.: Harvest Books, 2000. An excellent cross section of poems by the 1996 Nobel Prize–winning poet.

## WEB SITES

Polish News. URL: http://www.polishnews.com. America's leading Polish bilingual illustrated monthly on-line with extensive coverage of current events in Poland.

Warsaw Daily. URL: http://www.warsawdaily.com. A comprehensive daily newsmagazine in English with a useful archive search, powered by the World News Network.

Warsaw Voice. URL: http://www.warsawvoice.pl. A weekly newsmagazine in English covering Polish politics, culture, business, and entertainment.

# INDEX